GREAT REVIEWS FOR *JUST LISTEN*

"Who would benefit from reading *Just Listen*? I can't think of anyone who wouldn't—customer service staff, managers, salespeople, parents, you name it…"
—*The Chronicle Herald*

"Useful insights into opening anyone up—a recalcitrant vendor, a desirable prospect, a client dragging ass…. Goulston's words gave me sizable goosebumps."
—*Forbes.com*

"*Just Listen* is an excellent guide for learning how to break down barriers."
—*Pittsburgh Post-Gazette*

"The most useful (five-star) book on communicating…. Everyone can be a better communicator with the right knowledge, and this book makes learning interesting and easy."
—**Lindsey Novak, nationally syndicated "At Work" columnist**

"An impressive bag of tricks…. A guide that is as entertaining as it is useful."
—*Publishers Weekly*

"It's a measure of how contentious work relationships can get that the author, a psychiatrist, draws on hostage-negotiation techniques to instruct readers on how to deal with 'defiant executives, angry employees or self-destructing management teams'…. Mission accomplished."
—*Time Magazine*

"I read *Just Listen* on a weekend plane ride, started putting the lessons to work on Monday, and have been using them routinely ever since. I've already ordered copies for everyone in Mattel's senior leadership team and for each of my grown kids."
—**Bob Eckert, CEO and Chairman, Mattel**

"This book will help you turn the impossible and unreachable people in your life into allies, devoted customers, loyal colleagues, and lifetime friends."
—**Keith Ferrazzi, bestselling author of** *Who's Got Your Back* **and** *Never Eat Alone*

"Easy to read, easy to follow, and the results are astounding."
—**Marshall Goldsmith, bestselling author of** *What Got You Here Won't Get You There* **and** *Succession: Are You Ready?*

"A groundbreaking work that all leaders, present and future, should read, and more important, practice."
—**Warren Bennis, Distinguished Professor of Management, USC, and author of** *On Becoming a Leader*

"Goulston's book delivers on his promise. Read it and you will discover the secret to getting through to absolutely anyone, and I mean anyone!"
—**Mark Victor Hansen, co-author of** *Chicken Soup for the Soul*

"Full of lively, practical advice that will help you in every interpersonal interaction. Mark Goulston understands that communication is less about strategies and techniques than it is about making meaningful connections with people. His insights into human behavior are real gems."
—**Steven B. Sample, President, University of Southern California, author of the bestselling** *The Contrarian's Guide to Leadership*

"For far too many people, introspection is an elusive quality. But in his new book, *Just Listen*, Mark Goulston teaches us the power of introspection. He shows us how to look at ourselves and our relationships with others as a way to unlock powerful insights that can make us more effective at work and at play. You may think of yourself as confident and passionate, but could just as easily be seen by others as arrogant and impulsive. The gap between those perceptions is often the difference between success and failure. Goulston has written an important book to help us bridge that gap and to hone our introspective skills."
—**John Byrne, Executive Editor,** *BusinessWeek*

"Communication is not just *saying* something, it's being heard. Mark Goulston brings new meaning to 'getting through' to others. *Just Listen* is the indispensable guidebook for the journey to greater listening, caring, guiding, and fulfillment. We thank you, Mark."
—**Frances Hesselbein, Chairman and Founding President, Leader to Leader Institute**

"Mark Goulston provides the blueprint for connecting with people and building meaningful relationships in your personal and professional life. This is clearly Mark's most important work to date and a must-read for anyone focused on improving their personal effectiveness."
—**Wayne Gattinella, President & CEO, WebMD**

"Dr. Goulston brilliantly and practically shows us how to operational-ize the 'Golden Rule,' treating others the way we would want to be treated."
—**Michael Critelli, retired CEO and Chairman, Pitney Bowes**

"For most of my life, I thought I could talk my way out of any problem and into any party. *Just Listen* and Mark's advice helped me 'listen my way . . .' to the next level. This book is an instant classic and a must-read for any business leader."
—**Jason Calacanis, Internet entrepreneur, CEO, Mahalo**

"Want to master the one critical skill that's essential for success in both business and life? Read *Just Listen.* Goulston's simple, easy-to-apply techniques are powerful—and the results will amaze you."
—**Ivan R. Misner, Ph.D., Founder and Chairman, BNI;**
author of *The 29% Solution: 52 Networking Success Strategies*

"In this time of breathtaking developments in technology, it's easy to lose sight of what really connects us to one another. Mark Goulston's easy-to-absorb advice will help the reader build productive relation-ships at work, and grow closer to family and friends. This compelling mix of how the brain functions and how to break down barriers to effective communication will make you eager to apply Goulston's prac-tical suggestions. In other words, just read *Just Listen.*"
—**Tom Nelson, COO, AARP**

"*Just Listen* shows that it's much less important what you tell others than what you enable them to tell you. Goulston listened very well because this is not only one of the best books, but the easiest and most enjoyable one you could read on the power of listening."
—**Cathy Greenberg, author of *What Happy Women Know***

"To anybody who wants to improve their relationships at home, at work, or in the world, *Just Listen* is a must. Mark Goulston has written a masterpiece of a book that will improve every reader's life by making it much easier to communicate productively. Just read *Just Listen*."
  —**David Feinberg, M.D., M.B.A.; CEO, UCLA Hospital System**

"Mark's wisdom is not only knowledge-based, but useful. I have read hundreds of books, but few that I can actually apply to my business and relationships. Mark shares real issues and real usable solutions."
  —**Stephanie Allen, President**
  Food Development, Dream Dinners

"Goulston emanates deep caring like few I have known, and his ability to help us see ourselves without armor is both his gift and his gift to us. This book speaks straight from the heart, and it is now up to us to listen."
  —**Josh Waitzkin, author of *The Art of Learning***

"In a world where everyone wants to talk, the secret to success is the art of listening. Some great leaders are excellent speakers, and others are not—but all of them are great listeners. In this book, Mark Goulston deciphers the real secrets about listening. *Just Listen* will be one of the most influential books for the next ten years for the business world and beyond."
  —**Dr. Andreas Salcher, author of *The Talented Kid and His***
  ***Enemies* and *The Wounded Human*, and co-founder of the**
  Sir Karl Popper School

"Our parents were indeed right—we need to learn to listen. In *Just Listen* Goulston details in simple language how listening can help people achieve goals in their personal and professional journeys. It's about more than listening for listening's sake—it's about listening with a purpose."
  —**Dwayne C. Proctor, Ph.D., Senior Program Officer, Robert**
  Wood Johnson Foundation

JUST LISTEN

Discover the Secret to Getting Through to Absolutely Anyone

MARK GOULSTON

FOREWORD BY KEITH FERRAZZI
Author of *Never Eat Alone* and *Who's Got Your Back*

American Management Association

New York • Atlanta • Brussels • Chicago • Mexico City • San Francisco
Shanghai • Tokyo • Toronto • Washington, D.C.

Library of Congress Cataloging-in-Publication Data

Goulston, Mark.
    Just listen : discover the secret to getting through to absolutely anyone / by Mark Goulston ; foreword by Keith Ferrazzi.
      p. cm.
    Includes index.
    ISBN 978-0-8144-3647-9 (paperback)
    ISBN 978-0-8144-3648-6 (ebook)
    1. Business communication. 2. Interpersonal communication. I. Title.
    HF5718.G68   2010
    650.1'3—dc22

                                  2009014386

About AMA

American Management Association (www.amanet.org) is a world leader in talent development, advancing the skills of individuals to drive business success. Our mission is to support the goals of individuals and organizations through a complete range of products and services, including classroom and virtual seminars, webcasts, webinars, podcasts, conferences, corporate and government solutions, business books, and research. AMA's approach to improving performance combines experiential learning—learning through doing—with opportunities for ongoing professional growth at every step of one's career journey.

Printing number
10 9 8 7 6

To Warren Bennis, mentor, friend, and inspiration,
who taught me that when you "deeply listen" and get where people
are really coming from, and then care about them when you're there,
they're more likely to let you take them where you want them to go.

In Memory

"If you listen for hurt, fear, and pain or for people's hopes and dreams,
it is nearly always there. And when the other person feels you listening
and *FEELING* them, they will let down their guard and open their minds
and hearts to you."

   —Edwin Shneidman, pioneer in the field of suicide preven-
      tion, founder of the Los Angeles Suicide Prevention Center,
      and cherished mentor

And to my readers, that I may pass on this important
lesson to you.

CONTENTS

FOREWORD BY KEITH FERRAZZI   xiii
PREFACE TO THE PAPERBACK EDITION   xv
ACKNOWLEDGMENTS   xvii

SECTION I   THE SECRET TO REACHING ANYONE   1

1 WHO'S HOLDING *YOU* HOSTAGE?   3
The Persuasion Cycle   7
The Secret: Getting Through Is Simple   10

2 A LITTLE SCIENCE: HOW THE BRAIN GOES
FROM "NO" TO "YES"   14
The Three-Part Brain   15
Amygdala Hijack and the Death of Rational Thought   16
Mirror Neurons   19
From Theory to Action   23

SECTION II   THE 9 CORE RULES FOR
GETTING THROUGH TO ANYONE   25

3 MOVE YOURSELF FROM "OH F#@& TO OK"   27
Get Through to Yourself First   28
Speed Is Everything   29
The "Oh F#@& to OK" Process   30
The Power of "Oh F#@&"   31
The "Oh F#@& to OK" Speed Drill   32

4 REWIRE YOURSELF TO LISTEN   36
"But I Do Listen! . . . Don't I?"   38
How Well Do You Know the People You Know?   41

5   MAKE THE OTHER PERSON FEEL "FELT"   45
Why Does "Feeling Felt" Change People?   48
The Steps to Making Another Person Feel "Felt"   51

6   BE MORE INTERESTED THAN INTERESTING   55
The "Interesting" Jackass   57
Don't Just Act Interested—*Be* Interested   59

7   MAKE PEOPLE FEEL VALUABLE   64

8   HELP PEOPLE TO EXHALE EMOTIONALLY AND
MENTALLY   69
Moving a Person Away from Distress   70
Guiding a Person to Exhale   72

9   CHECK YOUR DISSONANCE AT THE DOOR   77
The Perils of Corporate Dissonance   83
When You Can't Avoid Dissonance, Anticipate It   85

10   WHEN ALL SEEMS LOST—BARE YOUR NECK   87
Show Them Your Neck, and They'll Want to
   Show You Theirs   89

11   STEER CLEAR OF TOXIC PEOPLE   94
Needy People   95
Bullies   99
Takers   102
Narcissists   103
Psychopaths   104
Mirror Check: Who's the Problem?   106

SECTION III 12 EASY-TO-USE TOOLS FOR
ACHIEVING BUY-IN AND GETTING THROUGH   109

12   THE IMPOSSIBILITY QUESTION   111

13   THE MAGIC PARADOX   116
The Cascade of "Yes"   117
A Trust-Gaining Move   119

14   **THE EMPATHY JOLT**   123
How It Works   126
When to Employ the Empathy Jolt   127
The Power of Analogy   129

15   **THE REVERSE PLAY, EMPATHY JOLT #2**   132

16   **"DO YOU *REALLY* BELIEVE THAT?"**   138

17   **THE POWER OF "HMMM. . . ."**   142

18   **THE STIPULATION GAMBIT**   150

19   **FROM TRANSACTION TO TRANSFORMATION**   155
Negotiating Versus Relating   156
What Question Would Make *You* Look Up?   161

20   **SIDE BY SIDE**   163

21   **FILL IN THE BLANKS**   170

22   **TAKE IT ALL THE WAY TO "NO"**   176

23   **THE POWER THANK YOU AND POWER APOLOGY**   180
"Thank You" Versus the Power Thank You   181
The Power Apology   183

**SECTION IV FAST FIXES FOR 7 CHALLENGING
SITUATIONS**   187

24   **THE TEAM FROM HELL**   189

25   **CLIMBING THE LADDER**   194

26   **THE NARCISSIST AT THE TABLE**   197

27 STRANGER IN TOWN   200
The Visibility Stage   201
The Credibility Stage   202
The Profitability Stage   203

28 THE HUMAN EXPLOSION   204

29 GETTING THROUGH TO YOURSELF   209

30 SIX DEGREES OF SEPARATION   215
Create One-on-One Situations   216
Make Virtual Allies   217
Reach the Gatekeepers   218

AFTERWORD   221
INDEX   223
ABOUT THE AUTHOR   231
KEYNOTES/WORKSHOPS   233

FOREWORD

Managers, CEOs, and salespeople often tell me, "Talking to so-and-so is like hitting a brick wall."

When I hear those words, I reply: "Stop hitting your head against the wall and look for the loose brick." Find that loose brick—what the other person really needs from you—and you can pull down the strongest barriers and connect with people in ways you never thought possible.

And that brings me to my friend and colleague Mark Goulston. Mark has an almost magical ability to reach everyone—corporate CEOs, managers, clients, patients, warring family members, even hostage takers—because he always finds the loose brick. He's a genius at reaching unreachable people and, in this book, you'll find out just how he does it.

I originally met Mark through his books *Get Out of Your Own Way* and *Get Out of Your Own Way at Work*. His books, his work, and, most important, Mark himself so impressed me that I pursued him and now we're business partners. He's one of the thought leaders at Ferrazzi Greenlight and a trusted adviser to me. After watching him work, I can tell you why everyone from the FBI to Oprah pays attention when Mark talks about reaching people: His techniques, simple as they sound, *really work*.

Oh, and don't be put off by the fact that Mark's a psychiatrist. He's also one of the best business communicators I've ever encountered. Put him in an office where everyone's at war or the sales team can't get buy-in from clients or morale and productivity are tanking, and he'll solve the problem—fast—in a win-win way where everyone comes out ahead.

If you'd like to achieve that kind of success, you'll find no better guide than Mark. He's brilliant, funny, kind, and inspiring, and his stories about everyone from unwelcome holiday guests to F. Lee

Bailey make his words as entertaining as they are life changing. So enjoy—and then use your powerful new skillset to turn the "impossible" and "unreachable" people in your life into allies, devoted customers, loyal colleagues, and lifetime friends.

Keith Ferrazzi

PREFACE TO THE PAPERBACK EDITION

Every day, I hear from people around the world who tell me that *Just Listen* has changed their lives. These stories delight and inspire me, because I truly believe that we can "heal the world one conversation at a time."

The letters and comments I receive come from people in every walk of life. I hear from CEOs and homemakers. From ministers, salespeople, teachers, and cops. From a college grad who scored an "impossible" job by listening. From a woman who saved her career by getting through to an unreachable boss.

Many of the letters I've received have brought me to tears. For instance, a mother in Omaha wrote to tell me that by using the tools in *Just Listen*, she'd reconciled with her adoptive daughter. And a man in India wrote to say that his father is now speaking to him after a 20-year silence.

And some readers made me laugh out loud. Here's one of my favorite comments:

"I just listened to my wife for a week now. She is extremely happy and not sure what really happened to me."

I'm humbled by these readers' words, and I appreciate their willingness to take the time and effort to reach out to me. And I'm grateful to them for confirming two things that I've learned from my own experience. The first is that simply *listening* to people will change both their lives and yours. And the second is that nearly all people—no matter who they are and where they live—will respond to true, agenda-less listening in an authentic and heartfelt way.

And here is another thing that readers tell me over and over again: Listening makes them care more about the people in their lives—and, by doing so, to come from the best and most worthy part of themselves. As one reader put it, "Listening has enabled me to demonstrate to myself that I'm a truly caring person. As a result, I finally feel as if I *deserve* to be successful and happy."

I hope that, like these readers, you will discover that the secret to getting through to people is not talking at them but listening to them. When you believe that people have an important story to tell, and let them tell it, you will be amazed at what happens.

And speaking of stories, I would like to close with a "Power Thank You" to all of the readers around the world who've so generously shared their stories with me. Thank you to new readers as well, for allowing me to share my ideas with you—I hope to hear your success stories soon.

—Mark Goulston

ACKNOWLEDGMENTS

Of all my books, I am proudest of and most enthusiastic about this one. Yet if it succeeds, it will be only because of the wise, caring, loving, critical, and generous input and support of many people.

First and foremost, I thank my readers, patients, clients, and customers, who entrusted me with their outer and inner hopes and fears and enabled me to pass on to you what I've learned from helping them.

I am also grateful to Bill Gladstone and Ming Russell, my supportive and steadfast agents at Waterside Productions, for their input and guidance and for hitting me upside the face when I gave in to a tendency to get in my own way. Many thanks are also due to Ellen Kadin, executive editor at my publisher, AMACOM Books, for having the love for this project and sound judgment to say when it was steering off path from delivering on its promise to my readers. The more useful and immediately usable tools you get from this book are largely due to Ellen's capacity as rudder and centerboard for this voyage. A big thank you as well to Sandra Vogel, Ph.D., senior leadership coach/consultant at Xavier University Leadership Center in Cincinnati, Ohio, for her invaluable help with the new edition of this book. I am grateful as well to Alison Blake, whose input aided me in clarifying my message, and to my ever-supportive former editor John Duff at Penguin Putnam.

Thanks are due as well to my close friends and PR specialists extraordinaire—Tom Brennan, Pam Golum, Cherie Kerr, Annie Jennings, and Paxton Quigley. I am very grateful also to Lynne Johnson at *Fast Company*, which carries my "Leading Edge" column and blogs; Marco Buscaglia at Tribune Media Services, which syndicates my "Solve Anything with Dr. Mark" column; and Arianna Huffington (*Huffington Post*), Matt Edelman (peoplejam), Kelly

Ja'don (Basil and Spice), and Marisa Porto (Divorce360) for featuring my blogs and content.

I am also greatly indebted to Keith Ferrazzi, John Kelly, Jeff Kaplan, Jim Hannon, Peter Winick, Kellee Johnson, Bo Manning, Chris Tuffli, and others I have met and continue to work with at Los Angeles–based Ferrazzi Greenlight. Keith originally wanted to call his killer bestselling book, *Never Eat Alone,* by a different title, *You Can't Get There Alone.* Boy, ain't that the truth! And his most recent book, *Who's Got Your Back,* reinforces how important it is to find people who'll pick you up, tell you the truth, and kick your butt (when you need it).

Because of these individuals' influence, I've opened myself to a world of people who have offered me their help. Of special mention are Martin Addison (Video Arts); Tony Baxter (Disney); Lee Canter; Jason Calacanis (Mahalo); Chris Coffey, Stephen Denning, Marty Edelston, and Marjory Abrams (Boardroom); Paul and Sarah Edwards and Bronwyn Fryer (*Harvard Business Review*); Dave Fuller (Costco Connection); Michael Gervais (Pinnacle Performer); Taavo Godtfredsen (Skillsoft); Katalina Groh (Groh Productions); Shawn Hunter (Skillsoft); Linda Kane (Bank of New York Mellon); Dave Logan (*Tribal Leadership*); Marty Nemko (NPR); Stacy Phillips (Phillips, Lerner, Lauzon and Jamra); Billy Pittard (Lynda.com); Tony Robbins; David Rock (*Neuroleadership*); Karen Salmansohn (*Bounce Back*); Heather Shea Schultz; Edwin Shneidman (UCLA); Leo Tilman (*Financial Darwinism*); Rebecca Torrey (Manatt); Josh ("Bobby Fisher") Waitzkin; and Peter Whybrow (UCLA).

Thanks are due as well to leaders whose most valuable resource is their time, but who nevertheless make time to talk with me: Scott Adelson (Houlihan Lokey); Sharon Allen (Deloitte); Jeffrey Berg (ICM); Angela Braley (Wellpoint); Mike Critelli (Pitney Bowes); Bob Eckert (Mattel); Werner Erhard; Jonathan Fielding (L.A. County Public Health); Jim Freedman (Barrington Associates); Bill George (former CEO, Medtronic and Harvard Business School); Marshall Goldsmith; Jim Goodnight (SAS); Peter Guber (Mandalay); Mark Victor Hansen (Chicken Soup); Frances Hesselbein (Leader to Leader Institute); Leonard Kleinrock (UCLA); Mike Leven (Georgia Aquarium); Jim Mazzo (Advanced Medical Optics); Ivan Misner

(BNI); Omar Noorzad (Tri-Cities Regional Center); Tom O'Toole (Hyatt); Bill Quicksilver (Manatt); Carla Sanger (LA's Best); Scott Scherr (Ultimate Software); Jim Sinegal (Costco); Sir Martin Sorrell (WPP); Bob Sutton (Stanford); Larry Thomas (Guitar Center); Raymond Tye (United Liquors); William Ury (Harvard); Duane Wall (White & Case); and David Wan (Harvard Business Publications).

My deepest thanks and appreciation go to my loving and supporting family, including my wife, Lisa, and children Lauren, Emily, and Billy, who serve as a never-ending insurance to prevent me from taking myself too seriously, and to my mother, Ruth, and brothers Noel and Robert and their families for their ongoing love and confidence.

And finally, a Power Thank You to the following people, living and deceased, whose ongoing support for the past decades has been instrumental to my learning and success: David Ackert, Sandy Archer, Rosanne Badowski, Joel Bagelman, Monica Ballard, Stan Barkey, Loretta Barrett, Jordon Bender, Hal Bergman, Davis Blaine, David Booth, Larry Braun, Eric Bruck, Shel Brucker, Jon Campbell, Stan Deakin, Susan Diamond, Kathy Doheny, Jim Dorsey, Albert Dorskind, Steven Drimmer, John Duff, Geoffrey Dunbar, Neil Elmouchi, Verena Florence, David and Gail Fogelson, John Fox, Sandy Fox, Ken and Lynn Franklin, Peter Frost, Gary Garbowitz, Larry Gerber, Selwyn Gerber, Harry Glazer, Roger Goff, Philip Goldberg, Cathy Greenberg, Gordon Gregory, Kevin Gregson, Arlen Gunner, Holly Gustlin, Cyrus Hekmat, Bruce Heller, Brian Hemsworth, Patrick Henry, Cheryl Hodgson, Paul Hynes, Grace Jamra, Annie Jennings, Preston Johnson, Marty Josephson, Joel Kabaker, Brian Katz, Jim Kennedy, Nancy Kent, Jeff Kichaven, John King, Brian Kurtz, Tracy Kwiker, Peter Lauzon, Mark Lefko, David Lerman, Mark Lerner, David LeVrier, Lisa Ling, Mark Lipis, Andy Ludlum, James Ludwick, Chris Malberg, Stephen Malley, Vicki Martin, Ken McLeod, William McNary, Frank Melton, Steve Mindel, Rebecca Nassi, Michael Parker, Kimberly Pease, Stacy Phillips, Martin Pichinson, Karen Pointer, Ken Potalivo, Scott Regberg, Tim Reuben, Mark Risley, Terri Robinson, Deborah Rodney, Patricia Romaine, Ivan Rosenberg, Lee Ryan, Millicent Sanchez, Myer Sankary, Suzana Santos, Gail Schaper-Gordon, Morrie Schectman, Greg Seal, Deborah Shames, Bill Sherman, Mark and Mia Silverman, Stan

Stahl, Robert Strauss, Ron Supancic, Eric Taub, Tony Trupiano, Tom Tyrrell, Monica Urquidi, Marcia Wasserman, Bob Weinberg, Joel Weinstein, Patricia Wheeler, Ward Wieman, and Halee Fischer-Wright.

THE SECRET TO REACHING ANYONE

Some lucky people seem to have a magic touch when it comes to getting people to buy into their plans, goals, and desires. But, in reality, reaching people isn't magic. It's an art . . . and a science. And it's easier than you think.

1
WHO'S HOLDING *YOU* HOSTAGE?

Good management is the art of making
problems so interesting and their solutions so
constructive that everyone wants to get to
work and deal with them.
—PAUL HAWKEN, AUTHOR,
NATURAL CAPITALISM

R ight now, there's someone in your life you need to reach. But you can't, and it's driving you crazy. Maybe it's somebody at work: a subordinate, a team member, a client, your boss. Or maybe it's somebody at home: a partner, a parent, a defiant teen, an angry "ex."

You've tried everything—logic, persuasion, forcefulness, pleading, anger—but you've hit a wall every time. You're mad, scared, or frustrated. And you're thinking, "What now?"

Here's what I want you to do: Think of this as a hostage situation. Why? Because you can't get free. You're trapped by another person's resistance, fear, hostility, apathy, stubbornness, self-centeredness, or neediness—and by your own inability to take effective action.

And that's where I come in.

I'm just an average guy—husband, father, doctor—but a long time ago, I discovered that I had a special talent. You could drop me into just about any situation, and I could reach people. I could persuade defiant executives, angry employees, or self-destructing man-

3

agement teams to work cooperatively toward solutions. I could get through to families in turmoil and to married couples who hated each other's guts. I could even change the minds of hostage takers and desperate people contemplating suicide.

I wasn't sure what I was doing differently from everybody else, but I could tell it worked. I knew I wasn't smarter than everybody else, and I knew my success wasn't just luck because what I did worked consistently, and it worked with all kinds of people in every type of situation. But *why* did it work?

In analyzing my methods, I found the answer. It turned out I'd happened on a simple, quick set of techniques—some I'd discovered on my own, and others I'd learned from mentors and colleagues—that create traction. That is, they pull people toward me, even if those people are trying to pull away.

To understand this, picture yourself driving up a steep hill. Your tires slip and slide and can't grab hold. But downshift, and you get control. It's like pulling the road to meet you.

Most people upshift when they want to get through to other people. They persuade. They encourage. They argue. They push. And in the process, they create resistance. When you use the techniques I offer, you'll do exactly the opposite—you'll listen, ask, mirror, and reflect back to people what you've heard. When you do, they will feel seen, understood, and felt—and that unexpected downshift will draw them to you.

The powerful techniques you'll learn in this book can move people rapidly and easily, often within minutes, from "no" to "yes." I employ them every day to fix broken families and help warring couples fall in love again. I use them to save companies on the brink of meltdown, get feuding managers to work together effectively, and empower salespeople to make "impossible" sales. And I use them to help FBI agents and hostage negotiators succeed in the toughest situations possible, when life and death are on the line.

In fact, as you'll find out, you have a lot in common with hostage negotiators when it comes to reaching the people who don't want to listen to you. That's why this book starts with Frank's story.

Frank is sitting in his car in a large mall parking lot, and nobody is coming near him because he's holding a shotgun to his throat. The SWAT team and the hostage negotiation team are called in. The SWAT team takes positions behind other cars and vehicles, trying to not agitate the man.

As they wait, they fill in the background details. They're looking at a man in his early thirties who lost his customer service job at a large electronics store six months earlier for yelling at customers and coworkers. He'd interviewed for several jobs, but didn't get any of them. He was abusive verbally to his wife and two young children.

A month earlier, his wife and kids moved in with her parents in another city. She told him that she needed a break, and he needed to get his act together. The landlord of their apartment kicked him out at the same time because they hadn't paid the rent. He moved into a shabby room in a poor section of the city. He stopped bathing and shaving and ate next to nothing. The last straw was the restraining order he'd received the day before he ended up at the mall parking lot.

Now the lead negotiator is talking calmly to the man. "Frank, this is Lieutenant Evans, I'm going to be talking with you, because there is another way out of this besides hurting yourself. I know you don't think you have any choice, but you really do."

Frank exclaims: "You don't know s***. You're just like everyone else. Leave me the f*** alone!"

Lieutenant Evans replies: "I don't think I can do that. You're here in the middle of a mall parking lot with a gun to your throat, and I need to help you find another way out of this situation."

"Go f*** yourself! I don't need anyone's help!" Frank replies.

And so the conversation proceeds for an hour, with stretches of silence lasting several minutes or more. As the information about Frank comes in, it becomes clear that he's not an evil person, just a very disturbed and angry one. The SWAT team is poised to "take him out" if he threatens anyone else with his gun, but everyone except Frank would like to end this peacefully. However, the odds of that don't look so good.

After an hour and a half, another negotiator, Detective Kramer, arrives. Kramer is a graduate of one of the hostage negotiation training sessions I've delivered to police and FBI hostage negotiators.

Detective Kramer's been briefed about Frank's background and the status of this negotiation and offers Lieutenant Evans a different suggestion: "Here's what I want you to say to the guy: 'I'll bet you feel that nobody knows what it's like to have tried everything else and be stuck with this as your only way out, isn't that true?'"

Evans replies, "Say what?"

Kramer repeats the suggestion: "Yeah, go on, say this to the guy: 'I'll bet you feel that nobody knows what it's like to have tried everything else and be stuck with this as your only way out, isn't that true?'"

Evans complies and when he says that to Frank, Frank too replies with: "Say what?"

Evans repeats it to Frank, who this time responds: "Yeah, you're right, nobody knows and nobody gives a f***!"

Kramer tells Evans, "Good, you got a 'Yes'; now you're in. Let's build on that." He adds a second question for the lead negotiator to ask: "Yeah, and I'll bet you feel that nobody knows what it's like to start every day believing that there's more chance that something will go wrong than go right, isn't that true, too?"

To that, Frank replies: "Yeah, every f****** day! The same thing happens."

Kramer tells Evans to repeat what he's heard and get an additional confirmation: "And because nobody knows how bad it is and nobody cares and because nothing goes right and everything goes wrong, that's why you're in your car with a gun wanting to end it all. True?"

"True," Frank replied, his voice showing the earliest signs of calming down.

"Tell me more. What exactly has happened to you? When was your life last okay, and what's happened since then to turn it to crap?" Evans invites.

Frank starts to recount the events since he was fired from his job.

When he pauses, Evans responds with: "Really . . . tell me more."

Frank continues describing the problems he's had. At some point, with guidance from Kramer, Evans says: "And all of that's caused you to feel angry? Or frustrated? Or discouraged? Or hopeless? Or what exactly?" Evans waits for Frank to pick the word that best fits how he feels.

Frank finally owns up to: "Fed up."

Evans follows up with: "So you felt fed up and when you got that restraining order, that was the breaking point?"

"Yeah," Frank confirms. His voice, once hostile, is quieter now.

In a few sentences, Frank's gone from refusing to communicate to listening and beginning to have a conversation. What just happened? The most critical step in persuasion—the step I refer to as "buy-in"—has begun. That's the step where a person goes from resisting to listening and then to considering what's being said.

What caused Frank to start listening and begin to "buy in" to what Lieutenant Evans was saying? That shift was no accident. The secret lay in saying the words that Frank was thinking but not saying. When the lieutenant's words matched what Frank was thinking, Frank leaned into the conversation and began to say, "Yes."

■ THE PERSUASION CYCLE

You probably don't find yourself in the types of situations that hostage negotiators handle. But on any given day, who are *you* trying to persuade to do something?

The answer is: nearly everybody you meet. Almost all communication is an effort to get through to people and cause them to do something different than they were doing before. Maybe you're trying to sell them something. Maybe you're trying to talk sense into them. Or maybe you need to impress them that you're the right person for a job, a promotion, or a relationship.

But here's the challenge: People have their own needs, desires, and agendas. They have secrets they're hiding from you. And they're stressed, busy, and often feeling like they're in over their heads. To cope with their stress and insecurity, they throw up mental barricades that make it difficult to reach them even if they share your goals, and nearly impossible if they're hostile.

Approach these people armed solely with reason and facts, or resort to arguing or encouraging or pleading, and you'll expect to get through—but often you won't. Instead, you'll get smacked down, and you'll never have a clue why. (How often have you walked away from a sales pitch, an office meeting, or an argument with your partner or child, shaking your head and saying, "What the heck just happened?")

The good news is that you *can* get through, simply by changing your approach. The techniques I describe in this book work for hostage negotiators in the most desperate situations, and they're equally potent if you're trying to reach a boss, a coworker, a client, a lover, or even an angry teenager. They're easy, they're fast, and you can hit the ground running with them.

These techniques are powerful because they address the core of successful communication: what I call the "Persuasion Cycle" (see Figure 1-1). In developing the Persuasion Cycle, I was inspired by the ground-breaking work and ideas of James Prochaska and Carlo DiClemente in their *Transtheoretical Model of Change* and by William R. Miller and Stephen Rollnick in their creation of *Motivational Interviewing*.

All persuasion moves through the steps of this cycle. To take people from the beginning to the end of the Persuasion Cycle, you need to speak with them in a manner that moves them:

- From *resisting* to *listening*
- From *listening* to *considering*
- From *considering* to *willing to do*
- From *willing to do* to *doing*
- From *doing* to *glad they did* and *continuing to do*

The focus, central tenet, *and* promise of this book, "the secret of getting through to absolutely anyone," is that you *get through* to people by having them "buy in." "Buy-in" occurs when people move from "resisting" to "listening" to "considering" what you're saying.

Ironically, the key to gaining "buy-in" and then moving people through the rest of the cycle is not what *you* tell *them*, but what

FIGURE 1-1 The Persuasion Cycle

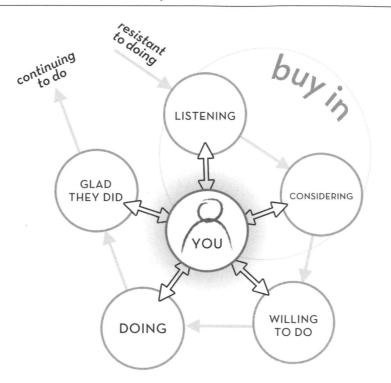

you get *them* to tell *you*—and what happens in their minds in the process

In the following chapters, I'll lay out nine basic rules and twelve quick techniques you can use to move people through different points on the Persuasion Cycle. Master these rules and techniques, and you can put them to work wherever you go in your career or personal life. They're the same concepts I teach FBI agents and hostage negotiators for building empathy, de-escalating conflict, and gaining buy-in to a desired solution—and when you know them, you won't need to be held hostage by another person's anger, fear, lack of interest, or hidden agenda. That's because you'll have the tools you need to turn the situation to your advantage.

As you read this book, you'll find multiple options for handling any situation. That's because while we're all similar in many ways, we each have our own way of doing things. The rules I outline in Section II are universal, but feel free to hand-pick the techniques in Sections III and IV that suit your personality and your life.

■ THE SECRET: GETTING THROUGH IS SIMPLE

There's nothing magic about the approaches you'll learn in these pages. In fact, one secret you'll discover is that reaching people is easier than it looks. To illustrate that point, I'll share the story of David, a CEO who used my techniques to turn his career around —and to save his family at the same time.

> David was technically competent, but heavy handed and dictatorial. His CTO quit David's firm, saying he loved the company but couldn't handle the boss. Employees underperformed to retaliate for David's abuse. Investors found him brusque and condescending, and they passed on the chance to invest in his company.
>
> I was called in by the board to see if David could be rehabilitated. I had strong doubts when I met with him, but I knew I had to make the effort to reach him.
>
> As David and I talked about his management style, I asked him on a whim, "How does your style play at home?"
>
> He replied, "Funny you should ask that." When I asked why, he responded, "I have a 15-year-old kid who's bright but lazy, and nothing I try works with him. He gets bad report cards, and my wife just coddles him. I love my kid but I'm almost disgusted by him. We had him evaluated, and he's got some kind of learning or attention problem. The teachers try to help him, but he just doesn't follow through with any of their suggestions. I think he's a good kid, but I just don't know what to make of it."
>
> On a hunch, I taught David some quick communication techniques and told him to test them at work and at home. We

scheduled a time to speak again a week later, but after just three days I received a message from him. It said: "Dr. Goulston, please give me a call at your earliest convenience. There's something I've got to talk to you about."

I thought to myself, "Oh God, what the heck happened?," and called him back. I was surprised to hear the emotion in his voice when he answered.

"Doc," he said, "I think you might have saved my life."

"What happened?" I asked, and he replied, "I did exactly what you told me to."

"With your board and people?" I asked. "How did. . . ."

He interrupted me. "No I haven't spoken with them yet. It was with my son. I went home and went into his room and said I needed to talk to him. Then I said to him, 'I'll bet you feel that none of us know what it's like to be told you're smart and not be able to use your intelligence to perform well. Isn't that so?' And his eyes started to water—just as you predicted."

David continued, "I followed up with the next question you suggested: 'And I'll bet sometimes you wish you weren't so smart, so we wouldn't have all these expectations of you and be on your case all the time about not trying harder, isn't that true too?' He started to cry . . . and my eyes began to water up. Then I asked him, 'How bad does it get for you?'"

David went on in a choked voice, "He could hardly talk. He said, 'It's getting worse, and I don't know how much more of it I can take. I'm disappointing everyone, all the time.'"

By this point, David told me, he was crying himself. "Why didn't you tell me it was so bad?" he asked his son. David told me with pain in his voice what happened next: "My son stopped crying and looked back at me with the anger and resentment that he must have been feeling for years. And he said, 'Because you didn't want to know.' And he was right."

"What did you do next?" I asked.

"I couldn't let him be alone in this." David said. "So I told him, 'We're going to fix this. In the meantime I'm going to bring my laptop and work on your bed and keep you company when you're doing your homework. I can't let you be alone when you're feeling so awful.' We've been doing it each night now for a few days, and I think he *and* we are starting to turn a corner."

He paused, and said, "You helped me dodge a bullet, Doc. What can I do in return for you?"

I replied, "Do unto your company as you just did unto your son."

"What do you mean?" he asked.

"You let your son exhale," I said. "When you did, he told you what was really going on underneath—and to your credit you handled it superbly. You have a load of people—from board members to your management team—who view you exactly as your son did, and they also need to exhale about their frustration with you."

David set up two meetings, one with his board and one with his executive team. He said the same thing to each group. He started off sternly: "I've got to tell you that I'm really very disappointed"—at which point both groups steeled themselves, preparing to take a tongue lashing—"I'm very disappointed in how I've jumped on all of you and then have been closed off to input from all of you, when you've steadfastly been trying to protect this company *and* me from *me*. I didn't want to listen, but I'm listening now."

David went on to share the story of his son. He concluded his remarks by saying, "I'm asking you to give me a second chance, because I think we can fix this. If you'll give me your input one more time, I'll listen and with your help find a way to implement your ideas."

His board and his management team not only decided to give him a second chance, they gave him a standing ovation.

What's the moral of this story? That the right words have tremendous power to heal. In David's case, a few hundred words saved his job, his company, and his relationship with his son.

But there's a second lesson here. Look at the two stories in this chapter, and you'll see that Detective Kramer and David used some of the same approaches to achieve very different goals. Detective Kramer kept a troubled man from killing himself, while David kept his company from firing him and mended the fractures in his family. The power of these techniques, and the others you'll learn, lies in the fact that they apply to nearly any person and any situation.

Why does a single set of communication tools have such universal power? Because while our lives and our problems are very different, our brains work in similar ways. In the next chapter, we'll take a very quick look at why our minds "buy in" or "buy out"—and why reaching an unreachable person depends on talking to the brain.

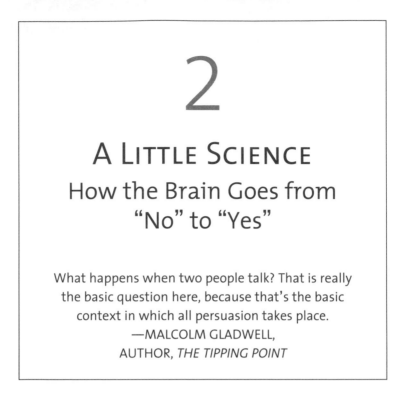

2

A LITTLE SCIENCE

How the Brain Goes from "No" to "Yes"

What happens when two people talk? That is really the basic question here, because that's the basic context in which all persuasion takes place.
—MALCOLM GLADWELL,
AUTHOR, *THE TIPPING POINT*

I think like a doctor, so I loaded an earlier draft of this chapter with drawings of brain parts and discussions of how the brain works. When I finished, I showed it to Ellen, my editor, thinking she'd say, "Wow. That's great."

Ellen quickly glanced over all the brain stuff. And then she said, pointedly: "Ick."

I got her point. Most people reading this book don't care about neurons and neurotransmitters and gray matter and white matter. If you're one of them, you just want to learn how to reach people. You don't care what happens inside their brains when you do.

But here's the thing: When you understand something about how the brain moves from resistance to buy-in, you'll have a huge edge—because no matter what your message is, you need to talk to the brain. That's why I teach a little brain science to hostage negotiators, CEOs, managers, parents, and anyone else who needs to reach difficult people.

However, I heeded Ellen's wise advice and took an axe to my first draft. Gone are the brain drawings and dry anatomy lectures. What's left? Three crucial concepts that will empower you to see what's happening behind another person's eyes when you're trying to get buy-in. Understand all three—the *three-part brain, amygdala hijack,* and *mirror neurons*—and you'll know all you need to know about the brain science behind reaching anyone.

■ THE THREE-PART BRAIN

How many brains do you have? It's a trick question, because the answer (as you probably know, if you took college biology) isn't one but three.

Your brain has three layers that evolved over millions of years: a primitive *reptile* layer, a more evolved *mammal* layer, and a final *primate* layer. They all interconnect, but in effect they often act like three different brains—and they're often at war with each other. Here's how each of your three brains behaves:

■ The lower reptilian brain is the "fight-or-flight" part of your brain. This region of your brain is all about acting and reacting, without a lot of thinking going on. It can also leave you frozen in a perceived crisis—the "deer-in-the-headlights" response.

■ The middle mammal brain is the seat of your emotions. (Call it your inner drama queen.) It's where powerful feelings—love, joy, sadness, anger, grief, jealousy, pleasure—arise.

■ The upper or primate brain is like *Star Trek's* Mr. Spock: It's the part that weighs a situation logically and rationally and generates a conscious plan of action. This brain collects data from the reptile and mammal brains, sifts it, analyzes it, and makes practical, smart, and ethical decisions.

As we evolved, the newer regions of our brains didn't vanquish the older parts. Instead, like the rings on a tree, each new region overlays the more primitive ones. The middle brain overlays the lower brain; the upper brain overlays the middle brain. And all three have power over how you think and act every day.

To a small extent, these three brains work together. To a greater extent, however, they tend to pull apart and function independently—especially when we're under stress. When that happens and the reptile or mammal brain takes control, the human thinking brain is eclipsed, and we shift into primal brain functions.

What does all of this have to do with getting through to people? Simple: To reach someone, you need to talk to the human upper brain—not the snake brain or the rat brain. You're in trouble if you're trying to gain buy-in from someone who's feeling angry, defiant, upset, or threatened because, in these situations, the person's higher brain isn't calling the shots. If you're talking to a boss, a customer, a spouse, or a child whose lower brain or midbrain is in control, you're talking to a cornered snake or, at best, a hysterical rabbit.

In this situation, your success hinges entirely on talking the person up from reptile to mammal to human brain—a technique I'll teach you later. For now, however, let's look at why the primitive brain can take over, canceling out all those centuries of evolution. The key: a region of the brain called the *amygdala*.

■ Amygdala Hijack and the Death of Rational Thought

Your amygdala, a small area deep in your brain, flies into action if it senses a threat to you—for instance, if a stranger approaches you in a dark parking lot. This threat doesn't always need to be physical; "fighting words," a financial scare, or even a challenge to your ego can light it off as well.

Your frontal cortex, the logical part of your brain, also goes on alert in situations where you sense a threat. However, this higher brain region wants to analyze the threat, and you don't always have time for that. That's why your body gives the amygdala the power to throw a switch, either directing impulses to or diverting impulses from the frontal cortex.

Sometimes when you're really scared, your amygdala instantly shuts out your higher brain, causing you to act on primitive instinct. Most of the time, however, the amygdala sizes up a situation before making its move. To understand this process, picture the amygdala as a full-to-the-brim pan of water on a stove. Heat this pan of water gently, and it can simmer gently for hours. Crank the heat up to high, however, and eventually the water will boil over catastrophically. Similarly, as long as your amygdala stays on "simmer" and isn't pushed into boiling over, you can continue to access your upper brain, which empowers you to pause, reflect, consider options, and make smart choices. When your amygdala hits the boiling point, however, it's all over.

We call this boiling-over point *amygdala hijack*—a term first coined by psychologist Daniel Goleman, the originator of the concept of emotional intelligence. The term "hijack" is appropriate because at that point (if you'll forgive me for detouring momentarily into another metaphor), your brain's intelligent and sensible pilot—the frontal cortex— is no longer in control. Instead, the snake is flying the plane. Your ability to reason drops drastically, your working memory falters, and stress hormones flood your system. Your adrenaline rush will keep you from thinking clearly in the next minutes, and it may take hours for the full effects to fade. Goleman no doubt was keen on this concept because when you undergo an amygdala hijack, your emotional intelligence goes out the window.

If you're trying to talk facts and reason with a person who's in full amygdala hijack, you're wasting your time. But intervene *before* the amygdala hits the boiling point, and the person's higher brain can stay in control. (Think of this as adding salt to water as you heat it. When you do that, you raise the water's boiling point, and it can take more heat while staying at a simmer.)

Many of the techniques I'll teach you for dealing with angry, fearful, or resistant people do just that: prevent an amygdala hijack. When you do that, you'll be talking to the human brain, and your words will get through.

Years ago, shortly after my father developed Alzheimer's, my mother called one day and said, "Your dad is driving himself and me crazy. He won't go outside, take a walk, or even go for a ride. I need you to come and talk to him." My mother wasn't the type of person who easily asked for assistance from anyone, but clearly my father—or more accurately, his condition—was keeping her hostage.

I booked a flight the next day. And for two-and-a-half days, I listened, talked, cajoled, and tried all of my hostage negotiation training tricks on my father—to no avail. The night before I was scheduled to leave, he said, "Do me a favor. Don't visit again so soon." Turning to my mother, he added, "Both of you get off my frickin' back and leave me alone."

I didn't sleep much that night, devastated that I—the shrink who could get through to anyone else—had so totally failed in my mission to get through to my own father.

The next morning, I sat on the porch with my dad sitting next to me, both of us staring out blankly at the nearby golf course. And suddenly, it dawned on me that my father was teetering on the brink of an amygdala hijack every single day—and all of my lecturing and pleading was simply shoving him smack into one. So I did something different this time: I focused on pulling him away from the brink.

Letting go of my own agenda completely, I leaned over and simply said:

"So, Dad, how are you doing?"

And with that, my dad looked at me, then looked away, then looked back at me, and finally looked down at the ground. His eyes began to tear up, and he said, "I never thought my life would end this way."

"I understand," I said very gently. Then my dad, who was terrified of admitting that he was losing his mind, scrunched his face up with all the concentration he could muster and asked me: "Mark, what is Alzheimer's?"

It was the start of a long, hard, and loving conversation. This time, I listened . . . and he listened. And it ended with me leaning over and giving him a kiss, and with us taking a long walk together.

■ MIRROR NEURONS

You cringe when a coworker gets a paper cut and cheer when a movie hero gets the girl. That's because for an instant, it's just as if these events are happening to you—and, in a way, they are.

Years ago, scientists studying specific nerve cells in macaque monkeys' prefrontal cortices found that the cells fired when the monkeys threw a ball or ate a banana. But here's the surprise: These same cells fired *when the monkeys watched another monkey performing these acts.* In other words, when Monkey #1 watched Monkey #2 toss a ball, the brain of the first monkey reacted just as if it had tossed the ball itself.

Scientists initially nicknamed these cells "monkey see, monkey do" neurons. Later they changed the name to *mirror neurons,* because these cells allow monkeys to mirror another being's actions in their own minds.

The new name is more accurate, because we're finding that humans, just like macaques, have neurons that act as mirrors. In fact, studies suggest that these remarkable cells may form the basis for human empathy. That's because, in effect, they transport us into another person's mind, briefly making us feel what the person is feeling. In a 2007 article titled "The Neurology of Self-Awareness" in *Edge,* V. S. Ramachandran, a pioneer in mirror neuron research, commented, "I call these 'empathy neurons,' or 'Dalai Lama neurons,' for they are dissolving the barrier between self and others."

In short, these cells may prove to be one way nature causes us to care about other people. But look at mirror neurons from another angle, and new questions emerge. Why is it that we often tear up when someone is kind to us? Why is it that we get a warm feeling when someone understands us? Why is it that a simple caring "Are you okay?" can so move us?

My theory, which my clinical findings support, is that we constantly mirror the world, conforming to its needs, trying to win its love and approval. And each time we mirror the world, it creates a little reciprocal hunger to be mirrored back. If that hunger isn't filled, we develop what I refer to as "mirror neuron gap."

In today's world, it's easy to imagine that gap growing into a deep ache. Many of the people I work with—from CEOs and managers to unhappy spouses to clinically depressed patients—feel that they give their best, only to be met day after day with apathy, hostility, or (possibly worst of all) no response at all. In my belief, this gap explains why we feel so overwhelmed when someone acknowledges either our pain or our triumphs. That's why many of the most powerful techniques I'll teach you involve mirroring another person's feelings—even if you don't agree with them.

Here's an example from my own practice that illustrates the surprising power of this approach. It involves Jack, a highly intelligent paranoid patient I saw several years ago. Before coming to me, Jack had seen four other psychiatrists.

"Before we start talking," Jack said right off the bat, "I need to tell you that the people living above me keep making noise all night long, and it's driving me crazy." He said this with a wry grin that seemed odd at the time.

"That must be exasperating to you," I responded empathetically.

Smiling mischievously as if he'd caught me in a trap, Jack added: "Oh, I neglected to tell you that I live on the top floor of my apartment building and there's no access to the roof." Then he looked at me with a smirk reminiscent of a comic looking to get a rise out of an audience.

I thought to myself: "Hmm. I could say 'and so?' and trigger a confrontation. I could say 'tell me more,' and have him go into even greater detail about his paranoid delusion. I could say 'I'm sure that the sound appears quite real to you, but a part of you knows it isn't' . . . , but that's probably what the other four psychiatrists said."

Then I asked myself, "What's more important to me? To be a calm, objective professional giving him yet another of the reality checks that he's already received from my profession? Or, to try to help him, even if it means letting go of reality?"

I decided on the latter. And with that conclusion, I let go of what I knew to be the truth and said with full sincerity: "Jack, I *believe* you."

With that, he looked at me and paused for a moment. Then, startling me, he started crying, making the sound of a starving feral cat out in the night. I thought I'd opened up a real can of worms and questioned my judgment, but I just let him cry. As the minutes went by, his crying lessened, sounding less animal and more human. Finally, he stopped, blotting his eyes with his sleeve and wiping his nose with a tissue. Then he looked at me again, seeming ten pounds lighter as if he'd just relieved himself of a tremendous burden, and offered me a wide, knowing grin. "It does sound crazy, doesn't it?"

We smiled together at the insight he'd just gained, and he took his first step toward getting better.

What happened to allow Jack to begin to give up his craziness? He felt *mirrored* by me. In his experience, the world required him to mirror and agree with *it,* whether it was a doctor saying, "You need this medication," or a psychiatrist saying, "You realize that these are delusions, don't you?" In that scenario, the world was always sane and right, and Jack was always insane and wrong. And "insane and wrong" is a heck of a lonely place to be.

My accurate mirroring helped Jack to feel less alone. As he felt less alone, he was able to feel some relief. And as he felt that relief, he was mentally able to relax. As a result, he felt grateful and, with that gratitude, came a willingness to open his mind to me and to work with me rather than fight me.

Now, you're not likely to deal with many paranoid schizophrenics in the course of your daily life unless you're a psychiatrist. But you will deal, every day, with people who have "mirror neuron gaps" because the world isn't giving back to them what they're putting out. (My guess, in fact, is that this is a nearly universal condition of humankind.) Understanding a person's hunger and responding to it is one of the most potent tools you'll ever discover for getting through to anyone you meet in business or your personal life.

The hunger to be mirrored can go well beyond one-on-one conversations. I'm reminded of an incident 20 years ago. In it, I watched an unassuming and even bland speaker not only get through to an audience of 300 people, but be more effective at it

than his charismatic copresenter, who possessed a much more powerful personality.

I was attending a two-day conference on an intensive and highly effective form of brief psychotherapy. The meeting featured two
speakers, a Canadian psychiatrist and a British psychiatrist who
were copioneers in that field. Each would speak, present videotapes
of sessions with patients, and then elicit comments, questions, and
discussions.

Right out of the gate, it was clear that the Canadian speaker was
powerful, focused, hard driving, and easy to listen to. In contrast, the
second psychiatrist, although equally clear, was calmer, low key, *and*
British, and it took more effort to pay attention to him.

But over the two days, a curious thing happened. The Canadian
speaker launched into his presentations like a 747 zooming down the
runway to takeoff. The British guy was more like a twin-engine Piper
Cub making its way down the runway at a more leisurely clip. The
Canadian's enthusiasm caused him to always exceed the allotted
times for his presentations, running well into the times allotted for
breaks. This caused the meeting staff to shorten breaks and urge us
to get back in time for the next presentation. The fact that a significant number of members of the audience were becoming restless,
looking at their watches, and rushing through snack breaks had little
impact on the Canadian. He was going to finish what he had to say,
whether or not anyone listened or cared.

In contrast, the British psychiatrist began his talks by tapping
on the microphone and asking if everyone could hear him in the
back of the room. He was also acutely attuned to any clues that the
audience's attention span was drifting significantly. At those
moments, he demonstrated one of the most dramatic instances of
mirroring I can remember—and he did it with a large audience, no
less. He would literally be in mid-sentence, stop himself, and say:
"You've heard enough for now. Let's take a break and resume in ten
minutes."

At first these episodes seemed a bit off the wall, but by the end
of the conference, the audience had clearly shifted from being
wowed by the charismatic but rather full-of-himself Canadian to
deeply appreciating *and* listening to the Brit who'd taken the effort

to accurately mirror them. The British doctor had won over a whole roomful of people, and he'd done it effortlessly.

■ FROM THEORY TO ACTION

The brain science I've outlined in this chapter comes with an asterisk attached: It doesn't apply to everyone. On rare occasions, you'll meet people who are stuck in their reptile or mammal brains and can't think logically no matter how much you try to help them. (Many, but not all, fall into the category of "mentally ill.") And you'll meet some people who don't give a damn if you mirror their feelings or not, because they're sociopaths or narcissists who only care about you doing what they want—which is why this book also includes techniques for dealing with bullies and jerks.

In almost every case, however, the people you'll meet are willing to be touched if you can just break through the walls they've erected to keep from being hurt or controlled. In the following chapters, I'll tell you how to effectively mirror the emotions of these people, redirect them to their higher thought processes, and keep them from undergoing an amygdala hijack—all by putting a few simple rules and techniques into play. And I'll tell you how to keep your *own* brain under control, so you can stay cool and say the right thing instead of melting down under pressure.

When you can do all of these things, you'll be amazed at how easy it is to reach people—and you'll be amazed at the difference it will make to your job, your relationships, and your life.

THE 9 CORE RULES FOR GETTING THROUGH TO ANYONE

These days we're experts at "syncing"—getting different pieces of technology, to talk to each other. Few of us, however, are experts when it comes to syncing with other people. Master the nine basic rules in this section, and you'll know the secrets of connecting with anyone—at work, at home, and at every stage of your life.

Once you learn these rules, you'll be ready for Section III, where I'll teach you 12 quick ways to reach people at any point in the Persuasion Cycle. You can skip straight to those ready-to-use techniques, but I recommend that you read this section first. That's because the power of those techniques doesn't lie just in the words you say—

it lies in knowing why, when, and how to use them. And, as you'll see, it also lies in knowing how to lay the groundwork for your success.

3

Move Yourself from "Oh F#@& to OK"

The key to winning is poise under stress.
—PAUL BROWN, THE LATE COACH OF THE
CLEVELAND BROWNS AND CINCINNATI BENGALS

"Mark, I'm giddy with excitement," Jim Mazzo, CEO and chairman of Advanced Medical Optics, told me over the phone.

Jim is one of the most ethical and effective leaders I know. But even from such a remarkable man, his comment was astonishing — because on that day in 2007, Jim's company was in the midst of what most people would call a crisis.

Without waiting to ask his board for permission, Jim had just ordered a voluntary recall of an eye solution as soon as he learned that it could contribute to serious corneal infections. I'd called Jim to tell him how much I admired his action, which reminded me of James Burke's quick pulling of Tylenol when several bottles were found to be contaminated with cyanide.

Jim replied, "We are a great company, with total transparency, a set of values, and a code of conduct that we all respect and follow. I am thrilled because I know that this is one of those rare opportunities that will make both our company and me even better and I am excited to find out just how it will do both."

And then he said something that impressed me even more: "When bad things happen, if you resist the temptation to do anything that will make matters worse, you will discover valuable things about your company and yourself that you would never have learned had you not taken the hit."

That's sheer courage—and it paid off for AMO, which weathered the storm well and, in the process, enhanced its already sterling reputation as an ethical company deserving of the full trust of investors and consumers.

What's the difference between Jim and the business leaders who panic, lie, frantically attempt to cover up problems, or simply melt down when problems occur? He has the ability to rise above a crisis and do the right thing. That's because he's smart and ethical—and it's also because when trouble arises, he can quickly bring his initial fear response (a universal human reaction to crisis) under control. No doubt Jim starts out just as scared as anybody else when a crisis strikes, but he doesn't stay that way. Instead, his deeply held core values prevent his emotions from boiling over and causing him to do something hasty. As a result, while other people are tempted to hide or blame or lose control, he can think fast and communicate effectively.

■ Get Through to Yourself First

Getting your emotions under control isn't just a key to being a great leader like Jim. It's also the most important key to reaching other people, especially in times of stress or uncertainty. It's why a cool and controlled hostage negotiator can get through to someone who seems unreachable—and, conversely, why a person who's crying, whining, or yelling will turn off even a calm and empathetic listener.

In the chapters that follow, you'll learn lots of powerful techniques for changing another person. But one of the most powerful things you'll learn is how to be in control of your *own* thoughts and emotions—because most of the time, that's where successful communicating starts. Mastering the art of controlling yourself will change your life, because it'll keep you from being your own worst enemy when it comes to reaching other people in stressful situations.

Of course, not all personal encounters are stressful. But many are—and these are the ones that can make or break a career or relationship. What's more, stressful encounters are the ones that you're usually least ready to handle. Making a cold call, handling an angry client, going on a tough job interview, facing a furious lover, dealing with an insolent teen: all of these can affect your emotions to the point that you can't think clearly. And when that happens, you lose.

So the first and most important rule for taking control in a stressful situation is this: *get yourself under control first.* (That's why flight attendants instruct you to put your own oxygen mask on first before placing one on your child.) The good news is that getting yourself under control is simpler than you think.

■ SPEED IS EVERYTHING

In reality, you probably already know how to handle a tense situation intelligently. You know exactly how to go from attack mode to emotional mode to smart mode. Unfortunately, you probably don't know how to do it *fast.*

Instead, here's what usually happens. A few minutes after a stressful encounter, you calm down a little, your pulse slows, and you start breathing more slowly. A few minutes or hours after that, you probably gain enough self-control to start thinking your options through. And given still more time, you start thinking, "Hey . . . there's a smart way to handle this."

By then, however, it's often too late. You've already lost a sale, alienated a boss or coworker, or convinced a lover that you're bad news. Or you've missed the moment to make a perfect comment or a great first impression.

So what's the solution? In a stressful encounter, to keep from blowing a chance to reach another person, you need to get your thoughts and emotions under control in minutes—not hours. In short, you need to move almost instantly from your reptile to your mammal to your human brain. That sounds impossible, but it's not. In fact, with practice, you can do it in about two minutes. And when you do you'll have the advantage over everyone else in the room, because you'll be the only person who's actually thinking straight.

■ THE "OH F#@& TO OK" PROCESS

To understand how stress interferes with your power to reach people, you need to know the mental steps you go through in a time of stress or crisis. What's interesting is that even though every crisis seems different to you, your mind treats them all in pretty much the same way. It doesn't matter what the crisis is—a fender bender, a lost contract at work, an argument with a lover, or your teenager saying, "my girlfriend's pregnant"—you go through these steps in more or less the same order each time you're upset.

In a small crisis, you may start at a middle stage of this process. In a big one, you'll start at the bottom. I call the process "Oh F#@& to OK," and here's how it goes.

■ THE "OH F#@& TO OK" PROCESS ■

"Oh F#@&" (The Reaction Phase):

This is a disaster, I'm screwed, what the hell just happened, I can't fix this, it's all over.

"Oh God" (The Release Phase):

Oh my God, this is a huge mess and I'm going to get stuck with cleaning it up. Sh#%—this stuff always happens to me.

"Oh Jeez" (The Recenter Phase):

Alright, I can fix this. But it's not going to be fun.

"Oh Well" (The Refocus Phase):
I'm not going to let this ruin my life/my career/my day/this relationship, and here is what I need to do right now to make it better.

"OK" (The Reengage Phase):
I'm ready to fix this.

Now, here's the secret: When you become consciously aware of these stages and can mentally identify each one as it happens, you can manipulate your emotional response at each stage. As a result, you can speed shift from start to end in minutes. Some people, like Jim Mazzo, are probably born knowing how to do this—but if you weren't, you can learn now.

Clearly, I'm not saying you can solve a crisis in two minutes. You can't. What I'm saying is that you can *think your way through to the possible solution* that quickly. When you do that, you take yourself out of panic mode and into "solution" mode. As a result, you'll be able to say all the right things and avoid saying the wrong ones.

■ THE POWER OF "OH F#@&"

One absolutely crucial element in moving your brain from panic to logic is to put words to what you're feeling at each stage. You can do this silently if you're in public or out loud if you're alone, but either way it's a critical part of putting yourself in control fast.

Why? Research by Matthew Lieberman at UCLA shows that when people put words to their emotions—"afraid," "angry"—the amygdala, that little biological threat sensor that can throw the brain into animal mode, cools down almost instantly. At the same time, another part of the brain—part of the prefrontal cortex, which is the "smart" area of the brain—goes to work. This part of the brain appears to inhibit emotional responses so a person can think coolly about what's happening. And that's just what you want to do.

So surprisingly, now is not the time to lie to yourself and say, "I'm cool, I'm calm, it's fine." It's actually the time to say to yourself (at least at first): "Oh f#@&" or "I'm scared as hell."

◼ THE "OH F#@& TO OK" SPEED DRILL

While the simple act of naming the emotions you feel at each stage in a crisis is part of the solution, it's just the first step. That's why people who merely stand around yelling "Oh F#@&" in a crisis typically don't help to solve it. They've taken the first step out of their animal brains, but they aren't going any further for awhile.

So think of "Oh f#@&" as your starting point, but don't get stuck there. Instead, once you put words to your emotions and give your frontal lobes a toehold, begin working your brain up one level at a time from panic to control. Here's how to do it.

◼ THE "OH F#@& TO OK" SPEED DRILL ◼

"Oh F#@&" (The Reaction Phase):

Do NOT deny that you're upset and afraid. Instead, identify your feelings and acknowledge them, silently using words to describe your feelings. ("I'm really scared. I'm so afraid I could lose my job over this.") Say this out loud if you're alone, because the physical act of exhaling as you speak will help to calm you.

If you're in a position where you can get away for a minute or two, do so. If not, *do not talk to anyone else* during these first few seconds. You need to focus entirely on acknowledging and working up from your anger or panic. If you're in a position to keep your eyes closed for a minute or so, do so.

"Oh God" (The Release Phase):

After you admit the powerful emotion you're feeling, breathe deeply and slowly through your nose with your eyes closed and let it go. Keep doing this as long as it takes to let it go. After you've released your emotions, keep breathing and r-e-l-a-x. This will allow you to begin to regain your inner balance.

"Oh Jeez" (The Recenter Phase):

Keep breathing and, with each breath, let yourself go from Defcon 1 back down to Defcon 2, 3, 4, and 5. It may help to say these words as you go through this transition: "Oh f#@&!" "Oh God." "Oh jeez." "Oh well. . . ."

"Oh Well" (The Refocus Phase):

Start to think of what you can do to control the damage and make the best of the situation.

"OK" (The Reengage Phase)

If you've had your eyes closed up to now, open them. Then do what you need to do.

Initially, you'll find it tough to move rapidly from one of these steps to the next. That's because it's not instinctive for your brain to move instantly and fluidly from primitive to higher brain regions. (It's far more instinctive to wallow in "Oh f#@&" for minutes or hours.)

However, if you rehearse these steps in your mind and then use them in real life, you'll get better and faster each time. Give it six months, and you'll find that in the most stressful of situations, you're the one who takes charge and makes the right things happen.

This skill is particularly crucial to master if you're a person who falls prey to what I call "fearful aggression." This is something you sometimes see at dog shows, when a harmless-looking poodle or dachshund suddenly growls threateningly at a judge. The dog doesn't growl because it's a killer; it growls because it's scared senseless by the noise and commotion and falls headlong into "Oh f#@&" mode. As a psychiatrist, I see people trapped in fearful aggression all the time. If you often spot signs of this stress reaction in yourself—if your voice rises in stressful encounters, you sound strident or angry, and you feel the veins in your neck pulsing—then mastering the "Oh F#@& to OK" Speed Drill can save your job or your marriage.

You'll also find this skill invaluable if you're prone to tears when someone attacks you. By actively acknowledging the urge to cry ("Okay, this is the 'Oh God' stage, and I feel like crying at this point") rather than trying to fight it, you'll be in the powerful position of observing that option and deciding against it.

But even if you handle stress coolly and calmly, take time to master this skill—because you can handle stress even better. And often, getting yourself under control even a few seconds faster can mean the difference between reaching people and losing them.

The best example of coolness under fire I've ever seen involved former Secretary of State Colin Powell. In 1996, Powell was the keynote speaker at a national conference for a leading residential real estate company's top producers. By that point, he'd achieved tremendous popularity with the American public and was being considered as a presidential nominee.

I happened to be in the audience that day, and General Powell had me (and everyone else) in the palm of his hand. He urged the audience to give back to their communities. He spoke passionately of his gratitude for his family, childhood, and friends. And he exhorted us all to "do well by doing good."

At the end of his talk, he called for questions. Still feeling the warm glow of his inspiring words, we were totally unprepared for what happened next.

"General Powell," the first questioner said, "I understand that your wife once suffered from depression, had to take medicine, and was even in a mental hospital. Do you want to comment on that?"

You could hear all 8,000 people in the auditorium gasp at the inappropriateness—not to mention the cruelty—of the question. In the silence that followed, we all wondered how Powell would react to being blindsided. Edmund Muskie had thrown away his presidential hopes years earlier when a reporter asked about his wife's sanity, and he started to cry. What would Powell do under similar circumstances?

Here's exactly what he did. He looked at the questioner. He paused for a moment. And then he simply responded: "Excuse me—the person you love more than anyone is living in hell, and *you* don't do whatever you can to get her out. Do you have a problem with that, sir?"

I was in awe. His response was brilliant. It was calm. It was perfect.

And believe me: it wasn't the first thing General Powell wanted to do. For a split second, he probably wanted to walk down from the podium, grab the idiot who asked the question, and knock his teeth through the back of his head. Because that's what every one of us would want to do in his place.

But he didn't give in to anger (even though he had every right to). And he didn't cry, like Senator Muskie. Instead, he went from "Oh F#@& to OK" faster than I've ever seen anyone do it.

As a result, he reached me even more deeply than he had with his speech. He reached everyone in the audience and touched them to their core. And I have no doubt he reached the questioner just as powerfully as a fist in the face would have— without having to lift a finger to do it.

That's poise under pressure. And if you can achieve that same poise, it'll get you successfully through any stressful, high-stakes encounters that life hands you.

➡ *Usable Insight*
When you go from "Oh F#@& to OK," you go from being fixated on the way you are convinced the world should or shouldn't be, but never will be, to being ready to deal with the world the way it is.

➡ *Action Step*
Think back to the worst encounter you had in the past year with a colleague or loved one. Mentally walk yourself through the steps from "Oh F#@& to OK" as if you were reliving the incident. Then try the same technique the next time you fall into an argument with the same individual.

4

REWIRE YOURSELF
TO LISTEN

Life is mostly a matter of perception
and more often misperception.
—DAVE LOGAN, COAUTHOR, *TRIBAL LEADERSHIP*
AND *THE THREE LAWS OF PERFORMANCE*

"How many of you think you listen well, or at least moderately well?" I asked the audience of 500 real estate agents and brokers attending an annual national meeting.

Everyone raised a hand. I responded with, "How many of you would agree with me if I told you that *none* of you listen, *ever*?"

I paused and looked out at the audience. "Really? That's interesting. Not a single person raised a hand."

As a psychiatrist speaking to a group of hard-driving, cut-to-the-chase salespeople, I already had two strikes against me. First, I'm not a salesperson. Second, I'm a psychiatrist, and psychologist types and salespeople tend to raise each other's hackles. At that moment, with my audience probably thinking, "What an arrogant jerk," I was on the verge of a third strike.

I continued, "If I could prove that none of you listen, ever—*and* then show you how to correct this problem to make you more effective—how many of you would be interested in hearing more?"

Some of the audience raised their hands, but the look on peoples' faces communicated a clear message: "Okay, but you've got one shot and then you're toast."

Taking that shot, I said, "I'd like you to imagine an office assistant who doesn't get work done on time and often turns in work products with significant typos and other errors. Now, envision this person becoming defensive or angry or starting to cry if you try to address these failings."

I asked, "How many of you can think of someone who fits that description?" Nearly the entire room erupted with raised hands. ("Hey, looks like I got them back again," I thought.)

"Now without pulling your punches, what are the adjectives you would give such a person?" I asked. "I'll start the ball rolling with, 'sloppy.'"

"Lazy," "Undisciplined," "Lousy work ethic," "Typical millennial attitude" (that one got a confirmatory laugh), "Flake," members of the audience offered.

"Now," I said, "Imagine that it's Monday morning, and you ask, 'Did you get the papers ready for the messenger to take to the escrow company on Wednesday?' and the person says, 'No.' How many of you would again think something along the lines of 'loser'?" Hands went up all over the room.

"And what would you do next? Upshift emotionally, and start yelling or making demands? Complain to another agent or broker? Tell someone in your office you want the person off all your deals? Or just walk away in disgust, angry about the lousy quality of people in your company?" I asked.

I saw from their faces that I'd scored a hit. Clearly, many of these agents and brokers felt this frustration daily. And because I was mirroring them accurately, they were buying in to what I was saying . . . so far.

"Now," I said, "consider this. Suppose you say calmly, 'Why didn't you get them done?' and the person tears up and says:

'I actually did a lot of work on them over the weekend. I was all set to have them to you by this morning—and I *will* have them finished by the close of work today—but my grandfather, who has Alzheimer's, called me last night crying. He said my grandma had a major stroke and was being taken to the hospital by ambulance. My parents are both dead, and I'm the only person who can take care of my grandparents. So I dropped everything to take care of things, and I haven't slept the entire night. I know this isn't the first time I've screwed up—but it's been really tough taking care of both of them, and sometimes I get overwhelmed.'

"Would that change how you'd think about the person, and even how you'd respond?" I asked.

I heard murmur, murmur, murmur—the sound of shifting minds. "Of course," a number of the people replied.

"Well then I rest my case," I said. "You *didn't* listen. What you did is what we all do. You gathered some data from your early inter-actions with that person, jumped to conclusions, and formed per-ceptions that became hard-wired with words such as: 'lazy,' 'sloppy,' 'lousy work ethic,' and 'loser.' Those words became a filter through which you heard without listening."

The solution, I explained: Get rid of the filter. The stuff you think you already know about someone—"lazy," "loser," "whiny," "hostile," "impossible"—is, in reality, blocking out what you need to know. Remove that mental block, and you're ready to start reach-ing people you thought were unreachable.

■ "BUT I *DO* LISTEN! . . . DON'T I?"

Right now you may be saying, "Mark, all I do is listen. I listen in meetings. I listen to my coworkers. I listen to my spouse. I listen to my kids. Nobody ever shuts up."

And all that's true. But the problem is that while you're hearing, you're not *listening*, no matter how good your intentions and how hard you try. The reason: Your brain won't let you.

Remember the three-brain model I talked about earlier—mam-mal brain on top of reptile brain and human brain on top of mam-mal brain, with each one building on the one that came earlier in evolution? The instant judgments we make about people are simi-lar, because they too build on the past. That doesn't mean they're entirely wrong. (In fact, an initial "gut instinct" is often spot-on.) But it means they're not entirely right, either.

Our agents and brokers, for instance, immediately formed the opinion that their office assistant was a flake. It never even occurred to them—any of them—that the person's behavior had a different explanation. Why? Because all their lives, they've heard people who don't do a job well described as "lazy" or "slackers" or "flakes." Their colleague fit the pattern, so they applied the same labels—and those labels stuck.

Our perceptions get hard-wired in this rigid way for a simple reason: new knowledge builds on prior knowledge. We walk after we learn to crawl. We run after we learn to walk. We type effortlessly with our thumbs on a smartphone now because earlier we fumbled over that little keyboard for months. We can drive on autopilot because our brain remembers how we did it before.

Similarly, we size up a person instantly today because we're relying on everything we've heard or known about people in the past. Then we stick with that perception forever, and view every interaction with that person through its filter, because (again) it's what we've learned to do.

The problem is that while we think our first impressions of peo-ple are grounded solely in logic, they're not. In reality, they're a jum-bled mix of conscious and unconscious truth, fiction, and prejudice. Thus, from the very start, we're dealing with a fictitious creation—not a real person. Yet that first impression will color our feelings about another person for months or years to come. It'll also affect how we listen to that person, because we'll distort everything the person says to fit our preconceived notions.

■ How Many Filters Do You Have? ■

My friend Rick Middleton, founder of the Los Angeles–based communication company Executive Expression, uses the GGNEE model to describe how we put people in mental boxes before we even know them. Rick says that without realizing it, we categorize people instantly in the following sequence:

Gender

Generation (age)

Nationality (or ethnicity)

Education Level

Emotion

The sequence goes in this order because we see a person's gender, generation, and nationality first, hear the person's education level second, and feel the person's level of emotionality third. Keep the GGNEE model in mind, and it'll help you to spot subconscious filters that keep you from listening to—and reaching—other people.

Why do our minds work in this seemingly illogical way? Because much of the time, forming rigid opinions about people actually works. For instance, picture yourself boarding a crowded subway train. Your first impressions will tell you to stay away from the unwashed guy with a weird look in his eye, to sit by the old lady with the knitting basket, and to avoid eye contact with a hostile-looking teen in Goth makeup. Individually, each of these conclusions may be wrong—the Goth teen may very well be a brilliant and sensitive kid who needs a smile, the weirdo might be a harmless eccentric, and Grandma might be working for Al Qaeda—but you don't have time to analyze every person you meet. Instead, your brain builds on past experience and innate instinct to make quick decisions that may save your life.

So being a quick study isn't a bad thing. It only becomes bad if your quick study is inaccurate and leads you to the wrong conclusions. Unfortunately that happens to us every single day, because our brains are far better at leaping to conclusions than at stepping back to analyze them.

Perceiving is believing.
Misperceiving is deceiving—
And worse yet, prevents achieving.

The solution? *Think about what you're thinking.* When you con-
ιsly analyze the ideas you've formed about a person and weigh

these perceptions against reality, you can rewire your brain and build new, more accurate perceptions. Then you'll be communicating with the person who's really in front of you—not the fictitious character conjured up by your false perceptions.

To see this process in action, let's go back to the agents and brokers and their frustration over their "flaky" office assistant. Initially, most of these high achievers looked at such people rigidly: Shoddy work + excuses/defensiveness/blaming = flake = why bother even putting the time or effort into dealing with this person? But when I asked them to imagine that a "loser" might have a real reason for underperforming, it forced them to undo their hard-wired preconceptions. This act, in turn, forced them to create a new and more accurate understanding of the person they'd previously written off.

■ How Well Do You Know the People You Know?

"Mark," you may say, "That's all well and good. But how about the people I've known for years? I don't have false ideas about these people. In fact, I know them as well as I know myself."

My answer is: "No—you don't." Every week I deal with people who've lived together or worked together for decades. Often, these people don't have a clue about what makes each other tick. As a result, they mistake insecurity for arrogance, fear for stubbornness, and legitimate anger for "he's just a jerk." And they talk over, around, above, and against each other, without ever talking to each other—when all they need is to see what's really right in front of them.

Mr. and Mrs. Jackson were a good example. The two had been married to each other for 55 years, and they came to see me at Mrs. Jackson's insistence when their bickering reached such intensity that Mr. Jackson said coldly, "So, why don't you just leave?"

He'd said that many times before, but for some reason this time Mrs. Jackson became hurt and angry, packed his bags, and told him to get out. And this time she didn't back down. Mr. Jackson became a little panicky, because at age 82 he was very dependent on her. She said she'd only reconsider if they spoke to a counselor.

As I listened to them, it became clear that they actually still loved and were devoted to each other—but they'd stopped *liking* each other. After 20 minutes, I'd heard enough and said, "Stop!" to both of them.

Taken aback, they both fell silent. I said to Mrs. Jackson, "Do you know that your husband thinks marrying you was the best thing he ever did?"

Mrs. Jackson, caught surprised, said, "What?"

Without missing a beat, Mr. Jackson replied, "He is absolutely right. I supplied a house, but she gave me a home. Without her I wouldn't belong anywhere, and without her I wouldn't have any relationship with our kids because as an engineer, I am not the best communicator."

Mrs. Jackson looked dumbfounded. I turned my attention to Mr. Jackson and said, "And as for you, do you know that Mrs. Jackson thinks you're the best man she's ever known?"

I thought his jaw was going to fall off. "You've got to be kidding; she's always picking on me about something and telling me what to do and what not to do," he replied, flabbergasted.

"One hundred percent correct," Mrs. Jackson chimed in. "He is the best man I have ever known. True, he's not much of a communicator. But he never drank or fooled around with other women. And he worked hard at a job he didn't like to support me and the kids."

"But what about all that nitpicking?" Mr. Jackson interjected.

Mrs. Jackson replied, "I nitpick everyone. I'm a nitpicker. It drives our kids crazy too, but like I say, he is also probably the best thing that ever happened to me."

Talk about a couple who'd heard but not listened for decades! Sadly, they each felt merely tolerated when in fact they were each treasured. And look what happened when they finally **did** listen. They'd arrived so angry they could barely look at each other, but they left looking like two people who'd just fallen in love all over again. And all it took was a few minutes of real listening—something they hadn't done for over five decades.

After more than half a century of living together, the Jacksons knew thousands of things about each other. He knew what kind of ketchup she liked. She knew his childhood dog's name. They knew each other's health problems, bathroom habits, and favorite TV shows. And yet, when it came to the big stuff, they were complete strangers.

What does that tell you? That you probably know a lot less than you think you do about the people you want to reach, whether they're new in your life or people you've known forever. That what you *think* you know may be very wrong. And that reaching these people doesn't just mean opening their minds to you. It also means rewiring yourself so you can see these people as they really are.

So when you encounter problem people, realize that there's a reason they're behaving the way they do. It may be a new problem: a health scare, money problems, or job pressures. It may be a long-term problem: anxiety about not being good enough for a job, anger at not being respected, fear that you don't find them attractive or intelligent. And, yes: It may be that they're actually just jerks (but they're usually not). Open your own mind and look for the reasons behind the behavior, and you'll take the first step toward breaking down barriers and communicating with an "impossible" person.

➡ *Usable Insight*

If you want to open the lines of communication, open your own mind first.

➡ *Action Step*

Think of a "problem person" you don't know very well—someone who misses deadlines, blows up for no apparent reason, acts hostile, is oversensitive to criticism, or otherwise drives you nuts. Make a mental list of the words you'd use to describe the person: lazy, slacker, rude, jerk, etc.

Now, think of five secrets that could underlie the person's behavior (for example, "he's scared about a medical condition," "she's afraid that we don't respect her because of her age," "he's a recovering alcoholic and has some bad days," "she has post-traumatic stress disorder," "he got burned by a previous business partner and now he doesn't trust people"). Picture how your feelings about the person would change in each scenario you imagine.

Once you've used this exercise to open your mind, schedule a meeting or a lunch with the person—and see if you can find out the *real* reason for the problem behaviors you see.

5

MAKE THE OTHER
PERSON FEEL "FELT"

Self-actualizing people have a deep feeling of
identification, sympathy, and affection for human
beings in general. They feel kinship and connection,
as if all people were members of a single family.
—ABRAHAM MASLOW, PSYCHOLOGIST

ow much longer will this take? I've got better things
to do," grunted Hank, a gray-haired senior partner
at a prestigious L.A. boutique entertainment law
firm. I'd been called in to smooth out the relationship between Hank and Audrey, another senior partner. Audrey,
whose name preceded Hank's on the door, brought in most of
the firm's business. She was a good lawyer, but she really shined
as a rainmaker. Hank was a brilliant lawyer, but he'd rather eat
nails than schmooze to bring in business.

Unfortunately, rather than admiring and appreciating Audrey's
talents, Hank saw her as a loudmouth who frequently disrupted
the office with her excited outbursts after she'd been to an event,
appeared on television, or been interviewed by a magazine or
newspaper. Compounding the problem, Audrey wanted Hank's
admiration more than anyone else's in the firm, a carryover from
wanting respect from her father and never receiving it.

Hank's stubbornness stemmed in part from his background.
His mother, an emotionally overwhelming person, made life mis-

erable for his dad, his brother and sister, and Hank. When Hank left home, he swore that he'd never let anyone bulldoze him like that again. And Hank experienced Audrey as a bulldozer.

Since they shared cases, it was important that they work together more cooperatively, especially since their friction was spilling over to the rest of the firm and distracting everybody. My job: to get these two talking—and working—like a team.

At the moment, it was an uphill battle. The exchange between the two kept growing more heated, with Audrey's voice turning shrill and accusatory. Hank talked down to her in front of others, she said. And he snickered at her comments, making her feel humiliated.

Hank barked sarcastically, "Hey, she doesn't need any help from me to humiliate herself. She does a pretty good job of that on her own."

"See! What did I tell you?" Audrey chimed in.

Audrey's barrage continued for several minutes, with Hank looking alternately at the ceiling and his watch and saying on several occasions, "I *really* do have a lot of work to do. Can I leave yet?"

One of the services I provide to firms is what I call "Rent-an-Adult." At this point I certainly was the only adult in the room, and my patience for this exchange was growing thin.

As I listened to them, I realized that the issue wasn't Audrey's belief that Hank refused to listen to her. Even Hank's disrespect wasn't the whole answer. The key was that Audrey didn't feel *felt*. When I understood that, I asked myself what she was feeling, and it came to me.

I stopped them both. Then I looked at Hank and asked, "Do you know that Audrey feels that you find her utterly repulsive and disgusting a lot of the time?"

Bull's-eye. The flood gates opened, and Audrey started crying so hard that she could no longer engage in the stupid dance-of-death debate. Her deep sobbing revealed tremendous pain, but also relief and the awareness of "feeling felt."

With the tug-of-war abruptly ended, Hank became disarmed, and genuine. "Look," he said, "I don't think Audrey's repulsive or disgusting. She's an amazing rainmaker. She's one of the best business development lawyers in this town, which is something

I'm miserable at and feel miserable doing." He repeated, "I *don't* find her repulsive or disgusting. I even like her. It's just that sometimes she comes in and she's so hyper that she upsets the whole applecart of this office. And I . . . well, as you can tell . . . I prefer there to be more order." He looked at Audrey, whose tropical storm of tears was beginning to lift, and said, "Audrey, really . . . I don't think you're repulsive or disgusting. You just drive me frickin' nuts sometimes."

I looked at Audrey and asked, "And what redeeming characteristics do you see in Hank?"

She responded, "He's one of the smartest lawyers I know. Even if he's grumpy a lot of the time, he can size up what's wrong with any case and redirect any lawyer in the firm, including me, in a direction that will be more successful. I guess that's why it's so important to me that he thinks I'm a competent lawyer."

With those two seismic shifts, the tension started to lift and some of the warmth that these comrades-in-arms felt underneath their anger started to show through. In just minutes, they went from resistance ("I hate you") to considering ("maybe we could actually get along") on the Persuasion Cycle.

At that point, Hank added: "Audrey, you are a good lawyer"—and then he smiled, not able to give a compliment without taking something away—"it's just that you can be a real pain in the ass sometimes."

"You had to say that, didn't you?" I commented in response to Hank's sarcastic rejoinder.

In a moment of humility, Hank replied, "Just like a zebra can't change his stripes, neither can an asshole."

After this chance to get past venting and exhale, the two reached a point where they could commit to communicating better. For Hank, it meant being less caustic; for Audrey, it meant calming herself down before she came into the office following the adrenaline rush from some business development activity that had her all charged up. The result of their détente: a more cooperative and productive office and less time spent fighting each other.

Audrey's and Hank's story is so common it's almost universal. Look around your office, and you'll probably see at least a couple of smart, high-achieving people who can't stand to be in the same room with each other. Look higher, and you may spot a CEO who treats dedicated team members like enemies and has an astronomical staff turnover rate to show for it. If you're in sales or customer service, think about the clients who seem more interested in making you miserable than in getting service. In each case, look behind the façade and you'll probably spot a failure to "feel felt." You'll also find an opportunity to fix things.

■ WHY DOES "FEELING FELT" CHANGE PEOPLE?

Making someone "feel felt" simply means putting yourself in the other person's shoes. When you succeed, you can change the dynamics of a relationship in a heartbeat. At that instant, instead of trying to get the better of each other, you "get" each other and that breakthrough can lead to cooperation, collaboration, and effective communication.

The Cold War, in fact, may have ended on just such an empathic tipping point. In a now-legendary moment, President Ronald Reagan's talks with Soviet President Mikhail Gorbachev seemed to be at a standstill when Reagan looked behind his adversary's stubborn face to see a leader who truly loved his people. In a moment of brilliant simplicity, he invited Gorbachev to "Call me Ron" (as opposed to "Let's keep fighting president-to-president, digging our heels in and getting nowhere"). Gorbachev not only accepted the invitation, he joined Reagan in calling an end to the Cold War. That's a buy-in of global proportions!

One explanation for the effectiveness of making a person "feel felt" lies in the mirror neurons I talked about earlier. When you mirror what another person feels, the person is wired to mirror you in return. Say "I understand what you're feeling," and the other person will feel grateful and spontaneously express that gratitude with a desire to understand you in return. It's an irresistible biological urge, and one that pulls the person toward you.

Despite the power of this move, people often resist using it because they hesitate to poke around in other people's private feelings—especially at work. But if your relationship with another person looks like it's going nowhere, making that person "feel felt" is your best bet for achieving a breakthrough.

I used this approach recently in a meeting with John, a 45-year-old whose brusqueness bordered on hostility.

John was the CEO of a Fortune 1000 company. When his firm merged with a smaller one, the newly formed company needed to make major changes from the top down—and those changes created resistance from the bottom up. One of my specialties is helping firms manage the turmoil of transitions, so I'd come to offer my services.

Earlier, John had hired a big-name consulting firm to handle this same task. The firm made recommendations that looked wonderful on paper but proved completely unworkable. John escaped from that disaster unscathed, because he'd used a basic CYA strategy: Hire a prestigious consulting firm, and if it goes badly, you can say, "Don't blame me: After all, they're supposed to be the experts." The good news: He didn't get in trouble. The bad news: He still needed to solve the problem, and now he had a reduced budget—which is why he was speaking with me.

I knew this back-story, and I sensed the emotions that lay behind John's covert antagonism. In fact, I'd felt them a time or two myself. So instead of launching into my presentation, I paused and said, "You've been burned before, haven't you?"

"What?" retorted John, completely blindsided by my *non sequitor.*

I repeated myself, "You've been sold or told things before by consultants who didn't deliver on their promises. Maybe you even had some close calls explaining to a boss why your decisions didn't work out. And after you nearly escaped those, you said to yourself, 'I'll never put myself in such a vulnerable position again.' Now you don't know if what I'm offering will deliver the results I'm promising. Isn't that true?"

He nodded sheepishly in agreement, no doubt remembering some of those close calls and now surrendering to the fact that he couldn't hide from me.

"Hey, don't worry," I reassured him. "Everyone makes decisions they regret. *I've* made decisions I regret." He nodded slightly.

"So here's the deal," I continued. "Knowing what it's like to believe promises made by people who didn't keep them—*and* knowing how awful that felt—I would *never* do that to anyone else. And if I did do that to you, I think you should come after me. Now, that said, there are always bumps in the road as I work with a company. Often these relate to the company agreeing conceptually with something that turns out not to be workable. When that happens, I've found the best way to work through that to be. . . ." And I explained how we'd work through any rough spots.

Bottom line . . . I got the engagement.

How come? Something I know about seemingly confident people, and especially people who work in large companies, is that often they're more afraid of making a mistake than they are of wanting to do something right. (That's especially true for managers or CEOs in their mid-forties, and even truer if they're men.) That's because they're afraid of being pounced on if things go badly and afraid of the hit their self-esteem will take if they screw up.

When these people make a mistake and feel criticized or embarrassed from without and humiliated from within, they often promise themselves, "Never again will I put myself in a position to be beaten up like this." This unconsciously holds them back when they have to make a new decision that might turn out to be a mistake.

It's critical to know this, especially in situations in which you make a clear, concise, and reasonable presentation to someone who nods in acceptance but then fails to agree to it. At this point most salespeople or managers try to elicit further objections that they can overcome. Sometimes that works, but often it doesn't. That's because what the other person is thinking but not telling you is, "I'm afraid—terrified—of making a mistake."

By addressing this dynamic head-on and showing that you understand and accept how the person feels and that you'd feel the same, you make these frightened clients "feel felt." When people feel felt, they feel less alone, and when they feel less alone, they feel less anxious and afraid—and that opens them up to the message you're trying to send. They shift from defensiveness ("Get away!") to reason, and they're capable of hearing your message and weighing it rationally.

■ THE STEPS TO MAKING ANOTHER PERSON FEEL "FELT"

You might think, "Mark, this is all easy for you to say or do. You're a psychiatrist with 30 years experience." My response is, "Don't kid yourself. You don't need a medical degree to do something this simple." Here's all you need to do.

1. Attach an emotion to what you think the other person is feeling, such as "frustrated," "angry," or "afraid."
2. Say, "I'm trying to get a sense of what you're feeling and I think it's _____ . . ." and fill in an emotion. "Is that correct? If it's not, then what *are* you feeling?" Wait for the person to agree or correct you.
3. Then say, "How frustrated (angry, upset, etc.) are you?" Give the person time to respond. Be prepared, at least initially, for a torrent of emotions—especially if the person you're talking with is holding years of pent-up frustration, anger, or fear inside. This is not the time to fight back, or air your own grievances.
4. Next, say, "And the reason you're so frustrated (angry, upset, etc.) is because. . . ?" Again, let the person vent.
5. Then say, "Tell me—what needs to happen for that feeling to feel better?"
6. Next, say, "What part can I play in making that happen? What part can you play in making that happen?"

This script isn't cast in stone; use these questions as a starting point, and go where your conversation leads. Here's an example:

> CARMEN, TRYING TO FIND OUT WHY HER EMPLOYEE DEBBIE IS STALLING ON A CRUCIAL NEW PROJECT: Debbie, I'm sensing that you have some strong feelings about me asking you to take on this project.
>
> DEBBIE: Well . . . yes, I guess I do.
>
> CARMEN: I'm trying to get an idea of what you're feeling wondering if you're feeling a little scared about try so new and different. Or maybe even a lot scared. Is

DEBBIE (STARTING TO VENT): I was afraid to say anything, but . . . you know I'm not an expert at graphics, and it's so much to learn all at once. And it's just so much pressure, and Johnny's babysitter just quit so things are crazy at home, and . . . I'm just feeling overwhelmed, I guess. I know it's a great opportunity, but I'm scared that I'll blow it.

CARMEN: I can see why that's a whole lot to handle at once. I'm wondering what needs to happen to make this easier for you. Would it help if I ask Theo to give you a little training in using InDesign? He's pretty good at it.

DEBBIE: That would really help a lot. I'd feel a lot more confident if I didn't need to figure everything out all by myself.

CARMEN: Great. I'll ask him. Is there anything else that would make taking on this project easier?

DEBBIE, RELAXING AND STARTING TO THINK POSITIVELY ABOUT HER NEW ROLE: I'd like to get a little formal training in graphics and layout if you want me to do more projects like this. Do you think there's some money for that in the budget?

Sometimes another person's response when you touch on a powerful feeling will surprise you.

Several years ago I spent months trying to schedule a meeting with a CEO, only to find him distracted and cold when we finally got together. Frustrated, I finally blurted out, "How much time do you have to meet with me?"

He looked at me with a look that said, "I don't know, but it's just about over right now!" I thought he was going to throw me out at that point, but he fumbled with his appointment book in an obviously offended manner and replied, "Twenty minutes."

I took a deep breath. "Look," I said, "what I have to say is worth your undivided attention, which you can't give me because there is something on your mind that is much more important than meeting with me. So here's the deal. Let's stop now at minute three and reschedule our meeting when you can give me all of your attention, but you take the remaining 17 minutes and make a call to take care of whatever is weighing on your mind, because it's not fair to your people, people outside like me, and even yourself to not be able to listen."

There was a pregnant pause and then he looked right at me —he was totally engaged now—and then his eyes started to water. He said, "You've known me for three minutes and because I'm a very private person about personal matters, there are several people within 20 yards of where we are sitting who have known me for 10 years and don't know what you know. There *is* something that is bothering me. My wife is having a biopsy, and it doesn't look good. She's stronger than me and told me that I would be better off going to work. So I'm here, but I'm not really here."

I replied, "I'm sorry to hear that. And maybe you *shouldn't* be here."

Then like a wet dog shaking off his drenched fur, He continued: "Nope. I'm not as strong as my wife, but I *am* strong. Served two tours of duty in Vietnam. I'm better off being here and taking care of business. You've got my undivided attention *and* you've got your full 20 minutes."

What's the moral of this story? It's easy to focus so intently on getting something from someone else—more work from a coworker, more respect from a boss, a sale from a client—that you lose sight of the fact that inside every person is a real person who's just as afraid or nervous or in need of empathy as anyone else. If you ignore that person's feelings, you'll keep hitting the same brick wall of anger, antagonism, or apathy. Make the person "feel felt," on the other hand, and you're likely to transform yourself from a stranger or an enemy into a friend or an ally. You'll get less attitude, less obstruction, and more support—and you'll get your message through.

If it sounds too simple to be true, try it. You'll be surprised.

 Usable Insight
Inside every person—no matter how important or famous—is a real person who needs to "feel felt." Satisfy that need, and you'll transform yourself from a face in the crowd to a friend or an ally.

 Action Step
Think of someone you're trying to reach who either makes excuses or pushes back in some manner. Put yourself in the person's shoes

and ask yourself, "What would I feel in this person's position? Frustrated? Scared? Angry?"

Approach the person, and say, "I need to talk to you about something. I was so busy feeling upset with you and then acting impatient and irritated that I stepped on your toes instead of walking in your shoes. When I stopped to do that, I thought if I were you, I'd feel frustrated (scared, angry, etc.). Is that true?"

When the person tells you what he or she feels, find out what's causing the feeling and what needs to be different for the person to feel better and achieve more.

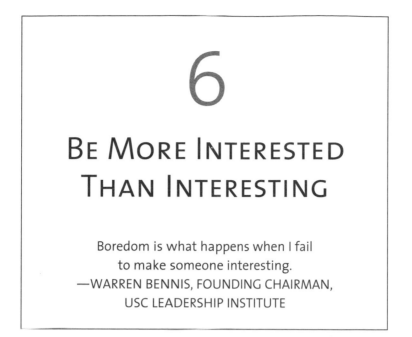

6

BE MORE INTERESTED
THAN INTERESTING

Boredom is what happens when I fail
to make someone interesting.
—WARREN BENNIS, FOUNDING CHAIRMAN,
USC LEADERSHIP INSTITUTE

Y ou're not just held hostage by the people who resist, bully, annoy, or get upset with you. You're also held hostage to your own mistakes when you fail to break through to people who either (a) don't know you at all or (b) don't act like they care to know you well.

Do you ever think in frustration: "I could get somewhere if only I could get this person *interested* in me?" That's exactly what I'm talking about. But here's the thing: embodied in your statement is the reason you're not getting through.

Why? Because you're focusing all your attention on what you can say to make that person think you're cool or smart or witty. And that's your mistake, because you've got it backward. To figure out why, look at what two of the world's most successful people do.

"Deep listening" is one of the terms most often used to describe Warren Bennis, founding chairman of the Leadership Institute at the University of Southern California. Warren is one of the most interesting people you'll ever meet, but when you're with him—I don't care if you're the guy parking his car, or the CEO of Google—he is more interested in you.

I saw this talent recently when I was invited to a dinner with some of his close friends who were all smart, thoughtful, *and* driven. As the evening progressed, lively dialogue turned into heated debate. Back and forth, these brilliant people fired salvos at each other, eventually reaching a point where I heard much more talking than listening.

Through it all, Warren sat with rapt attention and said nothing. At one point during a lull in the conversation, when the debating parties paused to reload their verbal ammunition, Warren stepped in and said to the more unrelenting of the debaters, "Bill, tell me more about that point you made about that philosopher." By not entering into the debate and by inviting one of the participants to exhale, Warren changed the entire tenor of the conversation and made it better.

Jim Collins is also one of the most interesting people you could ever meet. He's the author of *Good to Great,* one of the most successful business books of all time. He's been published in 35 languages. He received the Distinguished Teaching Award from Stanford, and he's climbed El Capitan—which puts him in the major leagues of rock climbing. But in a December 1, 2005, *Business 2.0* article entitled: "My Golden Rule," Collins explained why his rule is *not* to tell these interesting facts to everyone he meets:

> I learned this golden rule from the great civic leader John Gardner, who changed my life in 30 seconds. Gardner, founder of Common Cause, secretary of Health, Education, and Welfare in the Johnson administration, and author of such classic books as "Self-Renewal," spent the last few years of his life as a professor and mentor-at-large at Stanford University. One day early in my faculty teaching career—I think it was 1988 or 1989—Gardner sat me down. "It occurs to me, Jim, that you spend too much time trying to be interesting," he said. "Why don't you invest more time being interested?"
>
> If you want to have an interesting dinner conversation, be interested. If you want to have interesting things to write, be interested. If you want to meet interesting people, be interested in the people you meet—their lives, their history, their

story. Where are they from? How did they get here? What
have they learned? By practicing the art of being interested,
the majority of people can become fascinating teachers; nearly
everyone has an interesting story to tell.

What wise men like Warren Bennis (and no doubt Dale Carnegie)
instinctively know, and what "smarter than wise" younger, ambi-
tious people like Jim Collins and yours truly are still learning, is
that the way to truly win friends and influence the best people is to
be more interested in listening to them than you are in impressing
them.

From a brain science standpoint, here's why: The more interested you are in another person, the more you narrow the person's
mirror neuron gap—that biological hunger to have his or her feelings mirrored by the outside world (see Chapter 2). The more you
do that, the more intrigued the person is with you in return, and
the more empathy the person feels toward you. So to be interesting,
forget about being interesting. Instead, be *interested*.

■ THE "INTERESTING" JACKASS

Here's another illustration to help you grasp how important this
rule is. Imagine that it's holiday time, the mail just arrived, and
you're sorting through a stack of cards. You open the first one and
out falls a letter. It says:

> *"Bob and I took the family to Machu Picchu this year—unforget-
> table!!! Now we're into ballroom dancing and artisan bread baking. Call
> us crazy, but we just weren't busy enough even with all our charity work.
> (Was I ever surprised when the hospital gave me their Volunteer of the
> Year award last month!) Bob just got promoted to vice president—the
> youngest one in his company's history. Jessie's soccer team took first
> place in the state tournament, and we nearly burst with pride when
> little Brandy got a standing ovation as the lead in* The Nutcracker—
> *she clearly has the family's theatrical genes! Hope you're fine . . . we'd
> love to catch up with you the next time we're in town. . . ."*

Next, you come to a card from another friend. Scribbled inside is this note:

> *"Hey—how's it going? Nate and I thought of you the other day when we spotted an old junker that looked just like that car you had in college. What did you ever do with that monstrosity? (And how did you ever get so many dates when you drove it?)*
>
> *We're hoping to swing through town someday soon and take you out to lunch. We'd love to see the kids, too. Did Lisa apply to Julliard yet? We listen all the time to that tape of her performance last year, and it gives me chills every time I play it. What an amazing voice—tell her we can't wait to see her on Broadway.*
>
> *As for us, the kids are fine and Nate and I are still working too hard and earning too little—but having fun anyway. Happy holidays—we miss you!*

Consider these two cards. The first people win the "interesting" game hands-down—right? I mean, it's no contest. They have money. They have cool hobbies. They're intelligent and well traveled, and they're clearly highly successful. The people who sent the second card probably lead mundane lives by comparison. In the "aren't we interesting?" game, they obviously should lose.

But they don't. They win—and they win big. Why? Because they're interested in *you.* As a result, you'll probably say "yes" if they invite you to lunch. And Couple #1? When they call, you'll most likely tell them, "So sorry—we're out of town that week"—and breathe a sigh of relief when you hang up. That couple's fatal flaw is that they're trying too hard to be interesting . . . and as a result, they come off as annoying jerks.

The same thing holds true when you talk to people in person. The more you try to convince people that you're brilliant or charming or talented, the more they're likely to consider you boring or self-centered. That's especially true if you step on their stories in a rush to work in your own.

Focusing your energy on making yourself sound interesting can backfire even more painfully if you're trying to reach people in the stratosphere: corporate CEOs and other high achievers. These people are secure in their own *interestingness,* and so are the people they admire. Try too hard to impress them, and just like the *nouveau riche*—whose garish displays of wealth irritate "old money" people—you'll annoy them and drive them away.

■ DON'T JUST ACT INTERESTED—*BE* INTERESTED

As the old joke goes, "You can't fake sincerity." You can't fake interest, either, so don't try. The more you want to influence and get through to discerning and successful people, the more sincere your interest in them needs to be.

Recently, I was having lunch with an insurance professional in his mid-thirties and a lawyer in her early thirties. He asked all the right questions: "Where are you from?" "How did you get into what you do?" "What do you like about what you do?" "What would be the best client for you?"

I was impressed with his questions, and the young woman answered them with enthusiasm. The only problem is that when he asked them, he didn't seem earnest. Instead, he seemed to be following a script he'd learned in a sales training course. He did well enough to win over the young and somewhat inexperienced woman who'd joined us, but more experienced senior clients, customers, and prospects—who typically have highly refined bullshit detectors—would have picked up his insincerity and eaten him for lunch.

So: How do you master the skill of *being interested*—and be sincere when you do it? The first key is to stop thinking of conversation as a tennis match. (He scored a point. Now I need to score a point.) Instead, think of it as a detective game, in which your goal is to learn as much about the other person as you can. Go into the conversation *knowing* that there is something very interesting about the person, and be determined to discover it.

When you do this, your expectation will show in your eyes and body language. You'll instinctively ask questions that let the other person fully develop an interesting story, rather than trying to trump that story. And you'll listen to what the person is saying, rather than thinking solely about what you're going to say next.

The second key to being interested is to ask questions that demonstrate that you want to know more. It's not always easy, of course, to get another person to open up so that you *can* be interested in what he or she is saying. In a business setting, the best way I've discovered is to ask questions like these:

- "How'd you get into what you do?" (I credit Los Angeles super mediator Jeff Kichaven with this; he says it never fails to start and keep people talking.)
- "What do you like best about it?"
- "What are you trying to accomplish that's important to you in your career (business, life, etc.)?"
- "Why is *that* important to you?"
- "If you were to accomplish that, what would it mean to you and what would it enable you to do?"

In personal relationships—for instance, at a party or on a first date—questions like these can often trigger a heartfelt response:

- "What's the best (or worst) part of (coaching your kid's soccer team, being away from home, etc.)?"
- "What person has had the biggest influence on your life?"
- "Is that the person you're most grateful to? If not, who is?"
- "Did you ever get a chance to thank that individual?" (If the person asks, "Why are you asking these questions?," you can say: "I find giving people the chance to talk about who they're grateful to brings out the best in them.")
- "I'd like you to imagine that life is perfect . . . okay, tell me—what do you see?" (I credit Los Angeles–based human resource specialist Monica Urquidi with this tip. If the person asks why you're asking this, say: "I find that learning about people's hopes and dreams tells me what's important to them—that's a good thing to know, don't you think?")

et new people, I try to engage in conversations in which ons that will cause them to say: "I *feel* x, I *think* y, I *did* or " (what I call FTD Delivery). I know that when people ask me questions that generate all three of these answers, I feel "known" by them in ways that I usually don't if we're talking exclusively about what we feel *or* what we think *or* what we did or would do. Much of who we are is composed of what we feel, think, and do, so when we're in conversations where we get to express all three, we feel more satisfied.

Eventually, one of your questions will click and you'll see the person lean forward eagerly to tell you something with enthusiasm or intensity. When that happens, do the right thing: Shut up. Listen. Listen some more. And then, once the person reaches a stopping point, ask another question that proves that you heard (and care about) what the person said.

For example, if the person tells you that her college math professor had a huge influence on her life and explains why, don't reply by launching into a speech about your own professors. Instead, follow up with a question like: "I'm curious—why did you decide to go to that particular school?" or, "Whatever happened to that professor? Do you still keep in touch?"

Another way to show you're interested is to summarize what the person is saying. For instance, is the person regaling you with the story of a nightmare vacation trip? If so, repeat back some of the money points of the story: "Holy cow! You broke your leg, and you still made the flight. Unbelievable." (Another good move, if the conversation offers an opportunity, is to ask for advice: "That's amazing—you grow all of your own herbs? Tell me: How do you keep your cilantro from bolting?" People love offering advice, because it makes them feel both interesting and wise.)

At some point, if you're doing this skillfully and sincerely, the other person—who's grateful to you for really listening, which almost *never* happens in this world—will probably turn to you and say something like, "And what about you?"

And that is the big win you're looking for, because at that moment the person will return your interest by being interested in *you*.

"I've got a question," I blurted out just before the moderator of the panel asked for questions, and even before I knew the question I was going to ask.

I'd come to attend a town hall meeting at the Staples store in the mid-Wilshire area of Los Angeles for one purpose. That was to ask the first question—one that he'd want me to ask, and one the audience would want to hear—to Tom Stemberg, Staples founder and CEO.

One of my business colleagues, Patrick Henry, a professor in the entrepreneurial school at USC and an expert in networking, says that one of the best ways to get through to a powerful person is to be the first one to ask a question after the person speaks to a large audience. As Patrick explains, the audience will appreciate your courage at being the one to break the ice—and the speaker will appreciate you for starting the ball rolling with a good question and for preventing the awkward pause that can occur when there's a call for questions and nobody speaks out.

The trick, however, is to ask the right question.

I'm pretty quick on my feet, having appeared as a guest on more than 200 television and radio shows, so the five seconds it took to get the microphone to me was more than ample time to formulate my question. I quickly thought, "What's a question the audience and I would want to hear and Tom would want to answer?" As soon as the moderator handed me the microphone—I felt like someone was handing me a baton in a race—I had the answer: "Mr. Stemberg, if you had it to do over, what is something that would have saved you a lot of hassles later on in your career?"

Tom Stemberg is a brilliant entrepreneur, but that day he looked a little like a fish out of water. However, after I asked my question he brightened, clearly accepting the challenge.

He replied enthusiastically: "I would have waited longer to get venture capital money. I didn't realize that when you come up with a great new idea and the venture community hears about it, you're inviting a lot of competition. If I had it to do over again I would have delayed that and made sure I had a better head start instead of having 25 competitors that we had to beat in the early stages of our company."

Someone else wanted to answer the question, but Tom was on a roll and grabbed the microphone back. "Another thing," he added even more enthusiastically, "we were later than our competitors at doing home and office delivery. We pride ourselves on customizing our products and services and we should have thought that women secretaries probably don't like to carry cartons of paper up several flights. So Office Depot got a jump start on us there, but we'll catch up."

And just as Patrick predicted, both the audience and Tom appreciated my breaking the ice with my question, and Tom spoke directly to me with his answers. That gave me a chance to follow up with him afterward and to write him following his talk so I'd be remembered.

My approach worked because I didn't do what most people would. I didn't ask a question designed to make me look cool or clever or witty. Instead, I asked a question that Tom would want to answer, and one that let him be interesting to his audience. And that took me from being a face in the crowd to being someone he might himself find—dare I say it?—*interesting*.

➤ **Usable Insight**
The measure of self-assurance is how deeply and sincerely interested you are in others; the measure of insecurity is how much you try to impress them with you.

➤ **Action Step**
First, select two or three people you consider deadly dull and make it your mission to discover something fascinating about them. Now, do the opposite. Select a person you find interesting . . . someone you wish liked and respected you more. When an opportunity arises at a party or meeting, ask questions designed to show the person that you're *interested* rather than *interesting*.

Bonus round: Are you married, or living with someone? If so, the next time you're home together in the evening, ask, "How did that (work project, cooking experiment, etc.) that you were going to do turn out?" This will show that you don't just care about the person but also take the extra care to know what's going on in his or her life—and be interested in it. And after you ask this question, stun your partner by actually paying attention to the answer.

7

MAKE PEOPLE FEEL VALUABLE

Everyone has an invisible sign hanging from
their neck saying, "Make me feel important."
—MARY KAY ASH, FOUNDER,
MARY KAY COSMETICS, INC.

I'm going to start this chapter by telling you something you already know. And then I'll tell you something that sounds crazy but isn't—really.

Ready?

Here's what you already know: People need to feel valuable. We need this almost as we need food, air, and water. It's not good enough for us to know in our own hearts that we're valuable; we need to see our worth reflected in the eyes of the people around us.

Making people feel valuable is different from making them feel felt or feel interesting, because you touch them in an even deeper way. When you make someone feel valuable, you're telling the person, "You have a reason for being here. You have a reason for getting out of bed every morning and doing everything you do. You have a reason for being a part of this family, this company, this world. It makes a difference that you're here."

When you make people feel important, you give them a gift that's beyond price. In return, they'll often be willing to go to the ends of the world for you. That's why, if your emotional IQ is high, you'll find ways to show the people you value—parents, children, a partner, a boss, a key coworker—how much they matter. You'll find ways to tell them that they make your world happier, funnier, more secure, less stressed, more entertaining, less scary, or just all-around better.

Now, I'm guessing that so far you're with me. Much of this is common sense, and you can see that it'll work. So far, so good.

But this was the easy part. Now I want to tell you something you might have trouble believing. I want to convince you that it's smart to go out of your way to make the annoying people in your life—the complainers, kvetchers, and obstructers—feel important, too.

You're probably thinking, "Are you nuts? Why would I want to make the people who screw up my life feel valuable, when they aren't?"

The answer is simple. One thing most of these high-maintenance, easy-to-upset, difficult-to-please people have in common is that they feel as if the world isn't treating them well enough. In essence, they don't feel important or special enough in the world, usually because their awful personality has gotten in the way of success.

In Chapter 2, I talked about how our brains "mirror" other people and how we want to be mirrored back. People who complain and cause problems typically have a serious mirror neuron gap, and the more other people avoid or ignore them, the worse it gets. Every day, they try to impress or overpower the people around them . . . and every day they fail to get the feedback they're seeking. They're starving for attention, and if they can't find a good way to achieve the sense of importance they crave, they'll look for a bad way. (Call it the Graffiti Rule.)

In short, these people are driving you crazy for a simple reason: They need to matter. Want them to stop driving you crazy? Then you'll need to satisfy that need.

Here's an example. A while ago, I was talking privately with a middle manager named Janet. During our conversation, Anita—an office assistant with a reputation for wasting other people's time—burst into the office to say, "I've got to speak to you now!"

After Anita left, following a long-winded rant about a minor problem, Janet complained to me about her frequent and unnecessary interruptions. Fearful of escalating the problem, Janet hesitated to say anything. Instead, she stewed silently while Anita vented.

I suggested the following: "When Anita comes into your office, let her speak a couple of sentences and then firmly say, 'Anita, what you're saying is much too important for me to give it less than my undivided attention, which I can't give you now because I'm in the middle of something that I've got to finish. So what I'd like you to do is come back in two hours when I will be able to give you all of my attention for five minutes, and then I can help you with what's on your mind. But in the meantime think of what you want to tell me, what you'd like me to do, and whether it's possible given the reality of our company. Also, think about whether it's fair to everyone it affects and whether it's in line with what we're trying to accomplish. Figure those things out, and I'll be happy to help make it happen.'"

A few days later I spoke again with Janet, who'd tried the approach I suggested. She told me that Anita never came back and that things had been running smoothly since.

I explained to Janet that many "problem people" who come in just to vent do so because they feel frustrated at not feeling important in the company. A superior telling them that they are important can go a long way to calming that upset feeling. I also explained that subordinates who want to complain often don't have solutions to their problems, so when you set that as a condition for continuing a later conversation—a perfectly reasonable request—they often choose to drop the issue.

This is a potent way to handle troublemakers at work, and it works equally well in your personal life. Just like annoying coworkers, quarrelsome neighbors or difficult relatives often act out because they want you to notice and appreciate them. (If they didn't feel that way, they'd behave.) So give them what they want.

To illustrate how this works, let's look at an almost-universal problem: the unpleasant relatives who turn your holiday dinners into a nightmare. You're stuck with inviting these people, but you know they'll drive the other guests insane by complaining, arguing, or sulking. An unsolvable problem? Not at all. This is where thinking ahead and using the "I" (as in "important") word can do wonders.

Here's what you do. Call each of your problem people a week ahead of time—or, if you're a woman with a male partner, see if you can get him to make these calls because it's even more disarming for a man to ask for help. Say to these people, "I'm calling to ask you a favor because you're a very *important* part of our holiday dinners. Many of us don't see or even talk to each other except at the holidays, and you never know who's really having a bad time with a terrible illness, a recent death, or some big financial problems. So these dinners can be very awkward. Since you're such a consistent and important guest, I was hoping you might be able to greet people when they come in and help pull them out of their shell by asking them how they and their family are doing and finding out anything new that's been going on with them."

Doing something so gracious, and also giving these people who feel so cheated by life the chance to feel important, is not only quite flattering—it's also disarming. Your guests will have trouble responding, "No thanks. I was planning on coming and ruining everyone's time like I do every year."

Then, when the night of the dinner occurs, greet each problem guest at the door, touch the person on the arm, and say, "I hope I can count on you to help make people feel comfortable after they arrive." Before the person can respond, say, "Oh, excuse me. I have to go take care of some things." Then leave your newly assigned goodwill ambassador to spread joy and sunshine. Surprisingly, he or she will probably do a good job of it.

Follow this plan at each holiday, and you might find that your problem is solved. In fact, your former problem person is likely to become a strong ally of yours ("At least *somebody* appreciates me!") and will do everything possible to make your events a success.

The moral? The good people in your life need and deserve reassurance that they're valued—and the annoying people in your life may not deserve it, but they need it even more. Give both of them what they want—a feeling that they matter—and they'll give you what you need.

➡ *Usable Insight*

Everyone competes for time, but no one should need to compete for importance.

➡ *Action Step*

Identify a person at work or in your personal life who constantly creates problems where none exist. The next time the person complains about a problem, say, "What you're saying to me is so important that I'd like you to take responsibility for coming up with a solution. When you have some ideas, call me, and we'll get together and go over your solutions. I really appreciate your help."

Next, identify several people you value who might be feeling neglected. Call or write them and let them know how they've made an important difference in your life, or give them a "Power Thank You" (see Chapter 23).

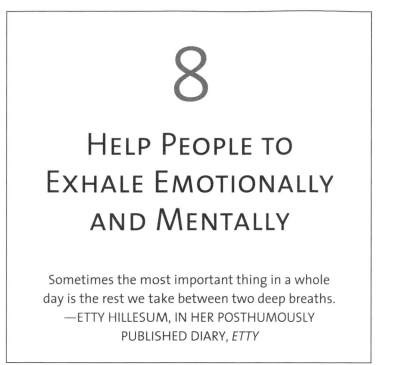

8

HELP PEOPLE TO EXHALE EMOTIONALLY AND MENTALLY

Sometimes the most important thing in a whole
day is the rest we take between two deep breaths.
—ETTY HILLESUM, IN HER POSTHUMOUSLY
PUBLISHED DIARY, *ETTY*

"Shh! Listen!" I said firmly to Alex, the stressed-out forty-something executive who'd been venting non-stop for 15 minutes about all the things he had to do and all the deadlines facing him and on and on.

He was startled, "Listen to what?"

"Listen to the *quiet*," I replied.

"The what?" he responded.

"To the quiet," I continued. "It's located between the noise in your head and the noise in your life, and right now it's screaming out to me and you to be heard."

"Huh?" he said, still confused.

"Close your eyes," I instructed, "and breathe slowly through your nose and in a little while you'll begin to hear it."

After several moments Alex began to tear up and then cry. This went on for five minutes, after which he slowly opened his blood-shot eyes. He had a smile on his face.

"What was *that* about?" I asked.

Alex chuckled wryly, "*That* is what I've been looking for all my life. And everything . . . and I mean *everything* . . . I do to get me there, takes me further away. That's a lot to think about."

He *did* go on to think about it—about the peace he'd felt in that moment, and what he needed to do to find more of it in his life. That's because he got the chance to exhale rather than merely vent.

▪ MOVING A PERSON AWAY FROM DISTRESS

Stress isn't bad. It causes us to focus, become determined, and test our mettle. It's when stress crosses over into *distress* that we lose sight of our important long-term goals and instead look for what will relieve us now. At that point, we're too busy looking for an emergency exit from our pain to be either rational or reachable.

Earlier, I talked about making people "feel felt." That's easier said than done, however, if you're dealing with people in distress. In these situations, the first step is to move people out of this state and into a state where their brains are capable of listening to you.

If you're trying to reach people in a state of distress, adding to their stress can be disastrous. This is the mistake that makes many hostage situations turn fatal—and it can also destroy a business deal or a relationship. Take the wrong step, and people on the brink of distress (or already over the edge) will respond in one of these ways:

- Shooting from the hip ("Oh yeah! Well, then, take that!"—maybe along with a stapler or even a punch getting thrown). That's the result of the amygdala hijack I talked about in Chapter 2, when the amygdala pulls the plug on the reasoning part of the brain and pushes the person to react in a hostile way.
- Venting ("You don't have a frickin clue about me"). You can't reach a person who's venting, because you wind up defending yourself or counterattacking.
- Suppressing ("Nothing's wrong," through gritted teeth). A person who chooses this route will close you out rather than letting you in.

But there's another option that people in distress can choose, if you show them the way: *exhaling.* Only exhaling enables people to experience and express their feelings—like draining a wound—in a way that doesn't attack others or themselves. It's the only response that relaxes stressed-out individuals and opens their minds to solutions from other people. That, in turn, offers an opportunity to resolve the source of the stress and prevent it from recurring.

When you give a distressed person *breathing room*—a place and a space to exhale—you don't just get the situation back to normal. You actually improve on it. That's because in addition to getting a person to calm down, you build a mental bridge between the person and yourself. And when you build that bridge, you can communicate across it.

Mr. Williams, a patient I encountered early in my career, had recently been diagnosed with lung cancer and had thrown out the last two psychiatric consultants who had tried to speak to him about his illness.

"You're going to love this guy," the oncology doctor told me sarcastically as we walked to his patient's room. I peeked in Mr. Williams's room and saw him sitting there steaming, seething, and ready to rip the head off of any shrink type who tried to talk to him about his illness. He wasn't handling his disease all that well—who could blame him?—and he clearly needed some kind of psychological assistance. He just didn't want any.

Envisioning him ripping me apart if I walked into his room and introduced myself as a psychiatrist, I came up with a different solution. I immediately went to Westwood Stationers and ordered a different name tag, replacing the one that said, "Mark Goulston, M.D., Psychiatry" with one that read, "Mark Goulston, M.D., Oncology." None of that soft-sounding specialty for me: I was going to act like a "real" doctor. I swear, when I put on that new name tag I even walked taller.

I entered Mr. Williams's room, trying to act like an oncologist instead of a psychiatrist, and said: "Hello, Mr. Williams, I'm Dr. Goulston, one of the new doctors on the oncology team." Then I began asking him questions about how he was doing and what his concerns were. However, I could see him sniffing as if he smelled a rat. I continued to talk, but it was clear he was on to me.

At one point our eyes locked and I knew he was going to tell me to get the hell out of the room. I realized that if I looked down or away I was lost, so instead, I continued to look into his eyes. As I did, I could see there was a lot going on underneath his baleful gaze. I don't know what possessed me, but I fired at him: "How *bad* does it get in there?"

He took my challenge head-on and fired back: "*You* don't want to know!"

I was temporarily at a loss for words, but then I somehow found these: "You're probably right—I probably don't want to know. But unless someone other than you knows and knows soon, you're going to go crazy!"

Surprised by my own audacity, especially with such a seriously ill man, I kept looking into his eyes, not knowing what he would say. He stared back at me with great intensity and then his face suddenly broke into a wide grin and he said: "Hey, I'm already there, pull up a chair."

He started to talk about how angry and afraid he was, and as he did, he exhaled even more. As a result of our talks, he began cooperating with the medical staff. His doctors told me he even required less pain medication. And I went from being the enemy to being a person Mr. Williams actively sought out as a sounding board for his fears and feelings.

■ GUIDING A PERSON TO EXHALE

When I first saw Mr. Williams, I didn't need to ask if he was in distress and heading toward meltdown. Even without his chart, I would have known. It was written all over him in body language: angry expression, rigid shoulders, crossed arms that said "get lost."

If you spot the same body language in someone you're trying to reach, don't try to get through with facts or reason. It won't work, because you're not going to get anywhere until the person exhales. Understand that you can't make the person do this—but you can make him or her *want* to do it.

Let's say, for instance, that you're confronting Dean, your boss, who's glaring at you across his desk with crossed arms and a thunderous brow. One of the best ways to get Dean to exhale is to get him to uncross his arms—both the real ones and the ones in his mind. Keep this in mind: Just as the hip bone's connected to the thigh bone, the crossed arms in a person's mind are connected to physically crossed arms. Get a person to uncross his arms physically, and you can get him to uncross his arms mentally.

To do this, ask Dean a question that creates tremendous emotion or passion in him. (That's why I goaded Mr. Williams, which seems counterintuitive with a very sick patient.) Words won't be sufficient to communicate what he feels, and he'll need to use his arms to emphasize what he says. That's why you often see people using their arms and hands to make a point even when they're talking on the phone.

When Dean uncrosses his arms and uses them to communicate, it will open a door in his mind. The problem is that when that door first opens, there's no room (yet) for you to get through it, because of the barrage that's coming out of the door at you. So here's what you do:

1. Give Dean plenty of time to express whatever he's saying. When people vent, whine, or complain, they're trying to prevent an amygdala hijack that could make them act out in some fight-or-flight way that could be far more destructive. Once they pick up speed, they don't want to be interrupted. (It's like finally having the opportunity to use the rest room after you've been stuck on the highway and not wanting to have to stop before you've relieved yourself!) The best thing to do when someone is venting, whining, or complaining is to avoid interrupting.
2. Don't take issue with anything Dean says, become defensive, or get into a debate.
3. After he vents, you'll both be exhausted. This is not to be confused with a relaxed state. The difference between *exhausted* and *relaxed* is that when you're exhausted, you feel empty and tired and you're not open to input. At this point, it may appear that it's your turn to talk—*but it's not.* Talking right now is the

rookie mistake that most people make. If you start to talk now, Dean will close down because he's too exhausted to listen.

Instead, pause after he's unloaded on you, and then simply say, "Tell me more." Doing this has several positive effects:

■ When it turns out you're not going to get into a debate with Dean, it disarms him. There's no need for him to fight you, if you don't engage in a fight.
■ "Tell me more" shows that you were listening and heard what really bothered him. It also lowers his paranoia that you're now going to come back at him for, in essence, dumping on you.
■ When you don't take issue with Dean venting at you, he will finally begin to exhale. You'll see it in his posture, in his face, and even in his breathing as he relaxes and lets go of his distress.

If you can allow Dean to exhale and then empathize with the upset he's feeling, he'll feel relieved, grateful to you, and in many cases willing to reciprocate. Why? Think back to the mirror neurons I talked about in Chapter 2. When you take a heavy burden off a person's shoulders, the person often wants to mirror your action by doing something similar for you.

Sometimes you can help a person who's venting to exhale by saying at some point, "Close your eyes, and just breathe." (I used this approach with Alex.) This triggers what Herbert Benson, a pioneer in the field of mind/body medicine, described as the *relaxation response*—the same response you're invoking if you practice meditation. In this physiological state, a person's heart rate, metabolism, breathing rate, and brainwaves all slow—the exact opposite of the fight-or-flight response. This triggers a calming chemical cascade that allows the person to exhale and "listen to the quiet." (I recommend this approach if you're dealing with a child or teen who's venting uncontrollably).

The biggest key to helping a person vent and then exhale, however, is to let it happen. Most people short circuit this process during the venting stage by becoming defensive ("I'm not the only one who's to blame here"), trying to offer solutions ("Well, maybe you should look for another job if you hate yours so much"), or getting nervous and trying to make things better ("Okay, I know it's been rough, but let's forget about all this for a few hours and go out to lunch"). Do not make any of these mistakes, because, like draining an infected wound, the job of getting a person to exhale isn't done until it's done. When it is, you'll earn your reward, in the form of a strong connection—one based on the powerful emotions of relief and gratitude—that you can use to get your own message across.

Here's a closing word for parents . . . especially those of you with teenagers. I offer it because getting your teen to exhale can save the sanity of everyone in your house.

If you've raised teens, you know that they often seem like alien beings—and in a sense, that's true. Compared to grown-ups, teens have a far stronger biological response to upsets and release more stress hormones. They also have different levels of the neurotransmitters dopamine and serotonin, making them more impulsive. Their neurons are still developing insulation and pruning excess connections—two processes that will eventually lead to mature thinking—and their decision-making circuits aren't fully developed yet. As a result, they're quick to move from stress into distress, they don't make judgments well, they can't communicate their feelings in a mature way, and they're quick to blow up, get moody, or say, "I hate you."

That explains them—but what about you? All of us make mistakes as parents—we're too overbearing, too protective, too anxious, too much of a doormat—and those mistakes can make our kids, who are already wired to be impulsive and quick to distress, respond in crazy ways that we call defiance, oppositional behavior, or just "being a jerk."

To see if this is happening in your household, give your sullen teenager a chance to tell you—and a chance to exhale. Wait until you're going for a drive and your child is captive in the car (since kids hate unsolicited heart-to-heart talks, which always feel like a lecture) and then ask these questions:

- "What's the most frustrated you have ever felt with your mom/dad or me?"
- "How bad was it for you?"
- "What did it make you want to do?"
- "What did you do?"

Then, if you get your child to answer these questions honestly, say (and mean it): "I'm sorry, I didn't know it was so bad."

Don't be surprised if you see tears of relief when you let your child exhale in this way. Better yet, those tears may be followed by the first nonantagonistic, nonconfrontational talk the two of you have had in a very long time. That's because exhaling will help your teen bring that strange, impulsive, moody brain under control—at least for a few blessed hours.

➡ **Usable Insight**
Forget about music. If you want to soothe the savage beast, get the beast to exhale.

➡ **Action Step**
If you're trying to reach someone who's suppressing his or her feelings, ask, "Have I ever made you feel that I don't respect you?" or "Have I ever made you feel that you weren't worth listening to?"

Be prepared for an emotional response to these questions, and don't interrupt the person or get defensive. Let the person vent and exhale. At that point, positive emotions will fill the hole left behind by the negative ones.

9

CHECK YOUR DISSONANCE AT THE DOOR

The most successful people are those who
don't have any illusions about who they are.
—BUD BRAY, AUTHOR, *IS IT TOO LATE TO
RUN AWAY AND JOIN THE CIRCUS?*

J ack was a civil tax attorney. By that, I don't mean that he did civil law; I mean that he was mild mannered, respectful, even tempered, and calm in his dealings with the IRS for his clients. He was very successful because of his incredible preparation, not because of the force of his personality.

Despite Jack's successful record, he came to see me because he wasn't getting as much business as some of his less competent peers. It didn't take me long to figure out why.

"When people hire a CPA to go up against the IRS," I said, "they unconsciously want to hire a gladiator. That's because they want to feel that whoever they hire could 'kill' for them if necessary." For all his talent, Jack just didn't come across as a killer. So even if he told people he could handle their cases against the IRS successfully, what they saw and heard in his manner didn't convince them.

Jack said he didn't think he could change his personality. "You don't need to," I said. "All you need to do is resolve the dissonance you create in other people by changing their perception of you."

I suggested that when he met with potential clients and sensed hesitation, he should add this: "Oh, by the way, if you decide to hire me to deal with the IRS you need to know that I am a 'killer,' but I am not a 'murderer.'"

I added that when they were startled by this statement, he should explain, "Many people who hire a tax attorney are scared that they've really messed up and the IRS is going to destroy them. They want an attorney who can go toe-to-toe with the IRS and win. Because I appear so even mannered, people may think that I can't 'kill' for them, if I need to. They would be making a mistake. I'm very prepared to 'kill' for my clients through a preparation that usually overwhelms the IRS, but I am *not* a murderer who takes delight in destroying someone just for the sake of doing it."

Jack tried this, with great success. He reported that using this approach caused more people to hire him—and it caused him to feel far more confident in his initial conversations with them.

What was the problem that had led Jack to seek me out? Dissonance. Dissonance occurs when you think you're coming across in one way but people see you in a totally different way. Jack, for example, thought he came off as quietly competent, but in fact he came off as timid until he made people see him in a different light.

Dissonance also happens when you think you're coming off as wise, but people see you as being sly—or when you think you're coming off as passionate, but other people think you're "over the top." When that happens, the result is buy-out.

Dissonance works the other way around, too: it occurs when you think you perceive someone else accurately, but the other person doesn't agree. There's hardly anything more annoying to another person than hearing you say, "I know where you're coming from," when you don't really have a clue. Often this happens when you aren't listening deeply enough to know what the other person is trying to communicate.

Dissonance makes a person stop thinking "What can this person do for me?" and start wondering, "What is this person planning to do *to* me?" It also keeps you and another person from connecting—or, from a neurological point of view, achieving mirror neuron empathy—because you're not sending the message you think you're sending. People can't reflect your confidence if it looks like arrogance. They can't mirror your concern if it sounds like hysteria. They can't mirror your calmness if they interpret it as apathy. And if you're misperceiving *them*—for instance, if you mistake their legitimate grievances for hysteria—the results can be fatal to a relationship.

Dissonance is a common culprit in marital disputes. Take Robert and Susan, a thirty-something couple who visited me. The two of them often fought over Robert's frequent failure to call to let Susan know that he'd be late for dinner, and about her being so controlling and rigid. (Sound like any people you know?)

As they talked, Susan frequently launched into accusations such as. "You *never* call to let me know about when you're coming home. You're so inconsiderate."

Robert would respond, "You're so pushy. You're just too controlling."

Finally I stopped them, and asked what they each heard each other saying. They both responded that the other person was saying, "I'm right, and you're wrong."

I responded, "Really? Are each of you actually saying, 'I'm right and you're wrong'?"

Susan looked at me and said, "No, that's not what I am saying." Robert agreed.

"So what *are* you saying?" I asked.

They both said, "What I'm saying is that, I'm not *always* wrong!"

"So each of you is actually defending yourself against the other's criticism much more than you're attacking the other person?" I asked.

"Absolutely," they both agreed.

"Hmm," I said. "So every time you try to protect yourself from being attacked, the other person feels as if you're *on* the attack."

Robert laughed, recognizing how this dynamic had played out time after time. He said ruefully, "Yeah . . . and we end up paying a shrink hundreds of dollars to sort it out."

The greatest single cause of dissonance is the fact that people behave their worst when they feel most powerless. So when a man or woman is yelling at a partner, or when a child and parent are yelling at each other, or when a boss is yelling at a subordinate, or when a customer is yelling at a customer service representative, it's because the person who's yelling feels that he or she isn't being heard or considered. In other words, the person who's yelling doesn't feel intimidating or scary (although that's what the other person perceives). Instead, the yeller feels powerless and small. This is dissonance at its most extreme, and it always ends badly.

Dissonance keeps you from reaching people, and it keeps other people from reaching you. As Susan and Robert discovered, dissonance can create fractures in a relationship—and as civil Jack discovered, it can stall a career. That's why you need to spot your own dissonance and correct it.

In my experience, the ten most common misperceptions that cause dissonance are the following.

BELIEVING YOU ARE:	WHEN OTHERS PERCEIVE YOU AS:
Shrewd	Sly
Confident	Arrogant
Humorous	Inappropriate
Energetic	Hyper
A Person with Strong Opinions	Opinionated
Passionate	Impulsive
Strong	Rigid
Detail oriented	Nitpicking
Quiet	Passive or Indecisive
Sensitive	Needy

But here's the challenge: How can you *know* how other people perceive you? The answer is simple but uncomfortable: Ask the experts—your own friends or relatives. This isn't fun, and you'll need to have a thick skin. But the quickest way to pinpoint your issues with dissonance is to identify two or three honest (or better yet, blunt) people who know you well and whose judgment you trust, and ask them to describe your worst traits.

Typically, even blunt people will hesitate to do this. To get them talking, don't say, "Do I have any characteristics that annoy or offend you?," because they'll just say "no." Instead, offer them a list and say, "I need you to mark, in 1-2-3 order, the top three ways I might rub people the wrong way." Here are the traits you can list:

- Arrogant
- "Hyper"
- Needy
- Overly opinionated
- Impulsive
- Rigid
- Nitpicking
- Passive
- Indecisive
- Demanding
- Hostile

- Stuffy
- Oversensitive
- Sly
- Untrustworthy
- Melodramatic
- Rude
- Shy
- Pessimistic
- Abrupt
- Excessively perky
- Closed minded

Odds are, if you ask three people to do this, you'll discover recurring themes. If two different people mark "abrupt," for example, believe them—even if you're sure you don't act that way. They'll probably couch their comments in terms like this: "Oh, you're not really that way, but. . . . Well, *some* people might see you as abrupt. I mean, not that *I* do. But I think some people could see you that way." If so, don't kid yourself: They're really saying, "I think you're too abrupt." And if your friends say that about you, it's probably true.

If you're feeling stoic, ask these same people to elaborate on the failings they identify. For instance, ask, "What do I do that strikes people as abrupt?" or "How often do I do that?" or "Would I seem less abrupt if I said such and such?" (Do *not* argue with them or hold their answers against them. Otherwise, you'll have to put a checkmark beside "closed minded" on your list.) With their answers in hand, study your own interactions with other people over the following days or weeks and try to spot the behaviors your critics pointed out. When you become aware of them, you can change them.

When you do this, you'll find it far easier to reach people. That's because dissonance makes people think uneasily, "there's just something about this guy that I don't like or trust," causing them to get stuck in resistance. Remove that dissonance, and their distrust often dissolves.

■ FEEDFORWARD ■

One good way to overcome the dissonance-creating traits you identify is to use what renowned leadership coach Marshall Goldsmith calls "feedforward." Here's how it works.

First, pick the behavior you most need to change. (For instance, "I want to be better at accepting criticism so people don't see me as defensive.") Now, approach anyone—your spouse, a friend, even a total stranger—and ask that person to suggest two things you can do in the future to change this behavior for the better.

Better yet, say to this person that you are looking to improve yourself as a boss, subordinate, friend, or whatever your relationship is with that person. Say that you'd like specific suggestions about something you could do differently going forward to improve the relationship from *the other person's* point of view.

If the person knows you, ask him or her not to talk about what you've done wrong in the past, but only about how you can do better from this point on. Listen to what the person says, and respond with only two words: "Thank you." Then repeat this process with additional people.

The great thing about this approach is that while most people are closed off to criticism about a mess-up in the past, nearly everybody is much more open to great ideas for future success. As Goldsmith says, "It works because we can change the future but not the past."

By the way, if you'd like to super-charge this feedforward process, read Goldsmith's book *What Got You Here Won't Get You There*. I don't gratuitously recommend books, but this one is a must for any manager (and I recommend it for any human). In the book, Goldsmith outlines 20 behaviors that can keep you from getting ahead and tells you how to address each one using feedforward and other techniques. Three of my favorite behaviors from the book are "adding too much value," "starting with 'no,' 'but,' or 'however,'" and "telling the world how smart we are." I love these because (a) you can just see the mirror neuron gap they create; (b) they are wonderful examples of not listening; and (c) I sometimes suffer from all of them. I'm not exaggerating when I say that if you have counter-productive or toxic behaviors you need to overcome, this book can change your life.

■ THE PERILS OF CORPORATE DISSONANCE

Just like married couples, companies can fall into the dissonance trap if they think they're sending employees one message but those employees hear something very different. CEOs who think their firms are great places to work often are stunned when I tell them their staffs find these companies stifling, unrewarding, unfriendly, or just plain awful. This is a bad situation because it's an open loop: There's no feedback to correct the dissonance, so it grows worse over time. The CEO typically grows bitter, decides that "these people are underproductive whiners," and implements punitive changes that make matters worse. The employees, in turn, grow even more annoyed or angry. Left uncorrected, this can lead to the worst-case scenario of a CEO giving people the least possible incentive to keep them working and those people doing the least they can to just hold onto their jobs, a situation that can bring a company to its knees.

After witnessing this scenario time after time, I developed a procedure called the PEP CEO Challenge to solve the problem. It's meant for corporate leaders, but you can tweak it to diagnose and repair dissonance in a smaller work group—or even in your own family, if they're willing. But one warning before you start: This tool is not for the faint of heart or for people who, in the words of Jack Nicholson in *A Few Good Men*, "can't handle the truth."

I created the PEP CEO Challenge with the help of the CEO of a children's book company (I'll call him Manuel). He ran a great company, but he knew it could be better. To find out how, I asked him to send out a memo to all his employees saying something along these lines:

1. I need your help in making this a better company. Anything you say to me will be totally anonymous.
2. Suppose you attended a dinner party and overheard someone describing his or her company as a "perfect 10" in the areas of

Passion, Enthusiasm, and Pride. How would you feel if you scored your feelings about your company lower? If it were me, I know I'd feel envious and feel less happy about where I worked.

3. If I were to ask you to score your own level of Passion, Enthusiasm, and Pride in regard to your job and our company on a scale of 1 to 10, what would you write down?

4. If you wrote down anything less than 10-10-10, what things would need to change, and in what ways, in order to raise those scores? Please give me your answers anonymously and please do not use this as an opportunity to single out individuals with whom you have a grievance.

5. When we receive your replies, we'll identify the most commonly reported suggestions for change going forward, tell you what they are and what we're going to do in response to them, and give you a time line for doing so.

    Thanks for helping us to turn this company into a place for which we can all feel Passion, Enthusiasm, and Pride.

I explained to Manuel that the PEP CEO Challenge sounds simple but reveals deep truths that can change a company's future. That's because:

■ Passion is about the vision of the company. People want to believe that they're doing an important job that makes a difference to their customers and clients, and puts a smile on their faces.

■ Enthusiasm is about execution. Even with a great vision, people lose their enthusiasm and fail to accomplish what they're capable of doing if their leaders are dropping the ball.

■ Pride is about ethics, because few people feel proud if their company is doing something dishonest. It's also about doing something meaningful, because as people grow older, leaving the world better than they found it becomes more important.

Manuel followed my suggestion and did this exercise with his company. People responded to the survey by saying they wanted better rewards for merit and fewer rewards for people who played office politics. They wanted less gossip and backstabbing and more cooperation. And when it came to the company's products, they wanted to deliver better on their mission statement, which was to create books that helped parents teach children how to succeed and be happy in a competitive and often cynical world.

Manuel committed himself to addressing all of these issues. The payoff: He increased his company's results and bottom line 40 percent in the next year. In particular, he took the suggestion about backstabbers and office politicians to heart, and he was able to ferret out the negative people and terminate them. More importantly, he doubled his own Passion, Enthusiasm, and Pride.

You can use this same tool to ask your employees, team members, directors, clients, or vendors to anonymously rate how much Passion, Enthusiasm, and Pride they feel about your services, products, company, and YOU on a scale of 1 to 10. Modify it a little, and —if you're feeling really brave—you can use it to ask your partner or kids how passionate, enthusiastic, and proud they feel about their family. The answers might not always be what you want to hear. But I can guarantee you they're what you need to know.

■ WHEN YOU CAN'T AVOID DISSONANCE, ANTICIPATE IT

So far I've talked about the kind of dissonance you can prevent. But not all dissonance is your fault and not all dissonance is avoidable. If you travel abroad or you work or live with people from many cultures, you'll eventually say or do something offensive to someone— even if you're trying your hardest not to.

You can't do a thing to avoid this. If you're not fluent in a language, the number of embarrassing mistakes you can make in trying to speak it is limitless. Or maybe you'll make a hand gesture that means "okay" or "stop" in your culture, but means something very different (and very bad) in another one. Or maybe you'll talk too long, or seem too abrupt, even if you're acting in a way that's polite in your culture. So there you'll be, radiating goodwill and politeness, and the other person will be thinking: "This person is a jerk who doesn't respect me."

This is no small problem. Entire business deals, and sometimes personal relationships, can founder on such small things as making too much (or too little) eye contact or picking up a roll with your left hand instead of your right.

Fortunately, preventing this problem is surprisingly simple. Being able to articulate awkwardness while being polite and respectful plays well in any culture, so here's all you need to do: Simply admit up front that you're likely to screw up. For instance, say, "I've read up on your culture and the differences between both of our cultures, and yet I am certain I will say and do things that may not fit. I'm not planning to, but it may happen—and the last thing I would want to do is embarrass you in front of your peers by making you have to explain my offensive behavior. If you tell me the most common things my culture does or doesn't do that offend your culture, I will try my very best to not act in those ways."

This type of humility totally disarms most people. It also erases dissonance even before it happens, because your advance apology will cancel out just about any mistake, from using the wrong fork to accidentally calling your host's wife a cow. So if you travel, and particularly if you participate in crucial cross-cultural business meetings, remember the art of "preemptive dissonance defusing"— and never leave home without it.

➥ *Usable Insight*
To paraphrase Warren Bennis, "When you really get where people are coming from—and they get that you get them—they're more likely to let you take them where you want them to go."

➥ *Action Step*
The next time you start sliding into an argument (especially if it's one of those chronic, simmering arguments that crops up constantly), stop and say to the other person, "Right now I feel like you're attacking me, and I'm guessing you feel like I'm attacking you. But in reality I think we're both defending ourselves. So I want you to know that I don't want to hurt you—and I know you don't want to hurt me. If we can start fresh with that agreement in place, I bet we can solve this problem together." When you do this, you'll replace your mutual dissonance ("this person is being a jerk") with mutual respect ("this person truly wants to solve our problem").

10

WHEN ALL SEEMS LOST—
BARE YOUR NECK

Don't be afraid of sharing your vulnerabilities.
Vulnerability doesn't make you weak,
it makes you accessible. Know that your
vulnerability can be your strength.
—KEITH FERRAZZI, AUTHOR,
WHO'S GOT YOUR BACK

Normally it takes work to get inside another person's head. When patients sit down across from me for the first time, I have no idea what makes them tick (or what makes them ticking bombs). In those first minutes they're mysteries to me, just as I am to them.

But that's not how it was with Vijay. He didn't come to my office. In fact, he was halfway around the world, in India. And I'd never met him. He'd e-mailed me "cold," after reading my blog and finding my e-mail address on the Internet.

But it didn't matter. The instant I read his e-mail, I knew exactly how Vijay felt. That's because 30 years ago I was standing in his shoes, and I was just as scared. And just like him, I didn't know what to do.

Vijay's message to me read:

I wish I had never been born, I wish that I could just jump off the roof of my house, I wake up wishing that I had never woken up from my sleep. I made a vow to myself that I actually wouldn't kill myself no matter what because I'm really scared of death, because I haven't accomplished anything so dying now would be more useless than staying alive.

I also wouldn't want to put a burden on my family. I don't want them to go through that terrible grief, or even worse, give the impression to my parents that all the hard work they did for my sister and me failed horribly.

That would be too much for them . . . but I simply don't have any interest in living, Doc. The main thing I think that triggered all these thoughts is that my O level exams start on 15 May. I've put a lot of pressure on myself to get high marks to make my parents happy. My dad always says to me that since I didn't do so well for my first two subjects, it is more important that I do well for the last three. I feel that if I get a B instead of an A, my parents won't love me anymore. . . .

Dr. Goulston, please e-mail me, I'm having all this trouble because I don't know who to talk to, in a calm voice that is. I'm begging you, Doc. . . .

I knew better than to brush off Vijay's fears about getting a B in school. Dozens of kids kill themselves each year over such small crises, and it's a particular risk in cultures like India where they take academic achievement very seriously.

So I wrote back immediately. I told Vijay I was sorry to hear how awful he felt. And then, knowing how alone he must feel, I told him my own story.

Early in medical school, I hit a point where I simply couldn't face continuing. I was passing my classes, but I didn't feel like I was learning anything because my mind shut down. I highlighted entire books hoping they would get into my brain by osmosis. I panicked at the thought of someday facing a patient and not knowing what I was doing.

So I went to tell my father I was dropping out. Like Vijay's dad, my father was someone who wasn't really in touch with emotions and saw them as excuses. When I told him about my decision, he looked at me with disgust and said, "So are you flunking out?"

I said, "No, I'm passing. But nothing I read seems to go into my brain or stay there." We started to argue, and then after a few minutes I gave up and just looked down at the ground.

He kept talking, making the case that I should just get tutors or do whatever it took to get through. Then he finished with, "So we're agreed, you'll just get some tutoring and you'll stay in school."

I thought to myself, "I can't go back. If I go back to school, something bad will happen. I'm afraid I'll go crazy or want to end it all."

So I just lifted my head and looked into his eyes and said from my heart, "YOU don't seem to understand. I'M AFRAID." It was the only thing I knew in my heart. I didn't even know whether I had the right to be afraid or what I was afraid of—other than it would be bad for me to go back to school. All I knew was that I was afraid.

After I said that, I started to cry. My tears had nothing to do with making excuses or feeling sorry for myself. They had everything to do with my fear, and a long-overdue need to get this off my chest and the monkey off my back.

It was my good fortune that under the tough exterior of a very logical, goal-oriented father was a dad who cared about his son. I half-expected him to say, "You're weak, you're disgusting, get away from me," which might have pushed me over the edge. But instead, he clenched his fists and then his anger melted away and he said, "Do whatever you need to do. Your mother and I will help you in whatever way we can."

This was the most powerful moment of my entire life, and it happened when I was at the lowest point of my life. It changed everything, because I was totally honest and true to my deepest feelings of fear and shame. So I told Vijay to do the same thing.

■ SHOW THEM YOUR NECK, AND THEY'LL WANT TO SHOW YOU THEIRS

Like most young people (men in particular), I once believed that earning respect meant never showing weakness—especially to my father. Instead, it meant hiding mistakes and covering fear with bravado. But I learned several things from this profound experience.

One is that people will forgive you and even try to help you if you're honest about a mistake. Another is that it's not telling the truth that makes people angry or disappointed in you. It's all the things you do to avoid telling them the truth.

I learned, too, that it's much better to reach out for help *before* you mess up. When you wait until you mess up and then ask for help, others may see it as a way to get out of being punished. Even so, it's better to reach out *after* a screw-up than to avoid reaching out at all.

Owning up to your feeling of vulnerability is empowering. It prevents an amygdala hijack that could result in rash decisions and seriously bad life choices. It allows you to exhale, rather than blowing up. Doing the opposite—pretending you're fine when your world is imploding—can be dangerous or even deadly.

But "assertive vulnerability" isn't just about blowing off steam; it's also about reaching people. To see why, let's get back to mirror neurons—the brain cells I talked about in Chapter 2—which allow us to feel what another person is feeling.

When you're scared or hurting or humiliated, but you're still in cover-up mode because you're afraid of losing another person's respect, here's what happens:

■   Your own mirror neuron gap widens. You don't feel understood because you *can't be understood.* That's because nobody has a clue what's going on with you. You're on your own, and it's a self-inflicted wound.

■   The person whose respect you're worried about losing (a parent, a boss, a child, a partner) can't mirror your distress and understand it. Instead, the person will mirror *the attitude you're using to mask your distress.* If you're using anger to cover up fear, you'll get anger in return. If you're using a "screw you" attitude to hide your feelings of helplessness, you'll get back "fine—screw you too."

When you bare your neck, however—when you find the courage to say "I'm afraid" or "I'm lonely" or "I don't know how to get through this"—the other person will immediately mirror your true feelings. It's biology; he or she can't help it. The person will know how bad you feel, and even feel the same pain. As a result the individual will want your pain (which is now, to some degree, his or her own pain) to stop. That leads to a desire to help . . . and a desire to help leads to a solution.

Interestingly, this is true even if you bare your vulnerability to people who don't like you very much. One of the jobs I'm asked to do most often is to handle jerks: corporate leaders who have tremendous skills but also glaring failings. Usually these people are rude, arrogant asses who cause good people to leave in droves and create such a toxic environment that nobody can function. They spend months or years tormenting their staff—making people feel small, weak, scared, unimportant, degraded, or humiliated—and when I come on the scene, these people are usually hoping for only one thing: revenge.

But then a remarkable thing happens. Once I make problem execs face their failings and tell them that their futures depend on fixing the problem, they agree and ask, "How?" And my first piece of advice is: Bare your neck. Tell the people you work with that you know you've been an ass. Tell them you'll do your best to reform. Lay it all on the table, and hope that they'll feel empathy.

And amazingly, most people do. In spite of everything the person put them through, they forgive. They even actively root for the reformed jerk. As a result, most of these ex-jerks get a second chance, and some even become good friends with the people they previously hurt.

Exposing your vulnerabilities can also create instant bonds strong enough to turn total strangers into friends. My partner Keith Ferrazzi uses the bare-your-neck approach at training sessions to get people to let down their guard and—as he puts it—"share the stuff that makes them human." He says,

> "I've heard so many touching stories recently from people who had the courage to try it. For instance, one young man had been on his sales job for six months but he wasn't making his quota. As a result, his compensation dipped significantly. It dipped so much, in

fact, that he had to sell his house and move his wife and two kids into a much smaller apartment. Another young guy said he has an autistic child whom he loves more than anything. He told us about the constant challenge of knowing that every hour he spends playing with that child, he's contributing to the child's development and keeping him from drifting away to the dark side. But he's always torn between how much time he has for that and having to work to pay the bills.

"That's some rough stuff they're going through. And many people would be too afraid to share those stories. But when you have the guts to share your vulnerabilities, two things happen. Inevitably, it turns out that your conversation partners have very similar vulnerabilities or problems in their lives. Secondly, they're so empathetic with you that they immediately want to help. They offer contacts or advice or just a pair of sympathetic ears. And instantly, you will have developed a more intimate relationship with your new friend, perhaps even more intimate than ones you have with some old friends."

You're even more likely to find support and empathy if you're baring your neck to someone who already cares deeply about you. Moms and dads in particular are biologically wired to care about you—no matter how brusque or demanding they may usually act. Reveal your wounds to them, and odds are they won't pour salt in them. Instead, they'll nearly always help you find a way to heal them.

All of which brings me back to Vijay. After reading my note, he went to his father and told the man about his fears of failing and disappointing the family. And—to his surprise—his father didn't melt down or say, "I'm disappointed in you." He didn't criticize. He didn't do any of the things Vijay feared. Instead, he understood. And he bared his own neck, by explaining that he knew he was sometimes impatient and that his own flaws got in the way of listening to Vijay. Together, they talked things out and came up with solutions. Vijay's dad would be less impatient. Vijay, for his part, would stop blowing his father's upsets out of proportion. And no matter how Vijay's exams turned out, they would both be fine.

After their talk, Vijay e-mailed me to say, *I didn't know that it was okay to be afraid. I was scared that my dad or anyone wouldn't accept me if I made a mistake.* Instead, he learned what we all find out at some point: Simply saying "I screwed up" or "I'm afraid" is often the wisest move to make when you need to reach another person.

In other words, assertive vulnerability isn't weakness—it's power.

➡ *Usable Insight*
When you're cornered and everything inside you makes you feel like baring your teeth, reach deeper into yourself, feel your fear, and bare your neck instead.

➡ *Action Step*
The next time you're afraid or in distress, don't pretend that you're not. Instead, identify the people you're trying to hide your emotions from—and then tell them the truth.

The next time you suspect that someone else is afraid or in distress, encourage the person to tell you about it. Then let the person know you respect him or her for having the guts to say "I'm scared" or "I made a mistake."

11

Steer Clear of Toxic People

A toxic person robs you of your self-esteem and
dignity and poisons the essence of who you are.
—LILIAN GLASS, PSYCHOLOGIST

I love connecting with people, and I go out of my way to do it. I'm a big fan of my partner Keith Ferrazzi's motto "Never Eat Alone," and I'm enormously grateful that nearly every new person I meet enriches my life.

But sometimes reaching out is a mistake. That's a lesson I finally had to learn myself, the hard way.

Four years ago, I had emergency, lifesaving surgery. During my recovery, I had a chance to think hard about some of the stressors in my life—stressors that made me less healthy than I could be and kept me from enjoying my life to the fullest. And while it may sound odd coming from a psychiatrist, the word at the top of my list of stressors was *people*.

Not people in general, however. Instead, the biggest stressors in my life were toxic people: the ones who were easy to upset and hard to please, who let me down time after time, who wouldn't cooperate or play fair, or who constantly made excuses and blamed other people.

I made a decision, at that moment in my hospital bed, to keep people like that out of my life in the future. I've kept that promise to myself and, as a result, I'm healthier, happier, and more successful in every area of my life. So as you're mastering my techniques for reaching people, I hope you'll make the same promise to yourself.

While this book is about connecting with the people who can make your life better, some people don't want to make your life better. Instead, they want to destroy it. Some of these people want to suck you dry, while others want to con you, thwart you, bully you, or make you the scapegoat for their mistakes. To save yourself, you need to strip these people of the power to hurt you.

There are three ways to do this. The first is to confront these people directly. The second is to neutralize them. The third is to walk away and make sure they don't follow you.

I know what you're thinking: "Easier said than done." Sometimes you're so entangled financially or emotionally that it's tough to do what I call a "jerkectomy." But painful or not, handling these people (or getting them out of your life entirely) is critical to your success and your sanity. Here's how to spot them—and how to defend yourself against them.

■ NEEDY PEOPLE

There's mildly needy, which isn't a big problem, and then there's drain-your-blood needy. It's the people in the second category you have to worry about.

Pathologically needy people can gut you emotionally or financially, or both. These are the people who send the messages: "I need you to solve all of my problems." "I can't function without you." "My happiness depends totally on you." "If you leave me, I'll die." Unlike *needful* people—who ask for help only when they need it and appreciate it when they get it—needy people demand constant help and attention, use emotional blackmail to get it, and offer gratitude only if it keeps you on the hook.

Perpetually needy people suck the life out of you, because no matter what you do for them, it's never enough. They don't lean toward you for occasional support; they lean *on* you until they crush you. And once they latch on to you, they'll almost never leave. (Why on earth would they?) Try to pry them off, and they'll grab on even tighter.

Needy people refuse to make decisions or handle issues on their own. They want you to spend hours holding their hand and helping them sort through their life problems. You'll handle one crisis only to find them weeping inconsolably over the next one. And you'll sink deeper and deeper in the quicksand each time you try to pull them out.

You'll also feel depressed and incompetent if you spend too much time with a needy person, because you'll knock yourself out and hear nothing in return except, "I'm still broken. I'm still sad. You've failed. You promised to save me but you didn't." That's a classic recipe for the mirror neuron gap I talk about in Chapter 2.

How can you tell if you're dealing with a pathologically needy person? If you suspect that you're trapped in this situation, rate the person in question on this 1 to 3 scale (1 = not at all; 2 = sometimes; 3 = almost always):

- Does the person whine?
- Does the person complain?
- Does the person come off like a victim?
- Does the person seem to be saying, "Feel sorry for me"?
- Does the person want to be pitied?
- Does the person cry or act deeply hurt when something doesn't go his or her way?
- Does the person attempt to make you feel guilty?
- Does it seem to you that the person is a bottomless pit whose needs can't ever be met?
- Do you want to avoid the person?
- Does your stomach get a knot whenever you receive a voice mail or e-mail from the person?
- Do you feel like yelling at the person: "Toughen up!"?

- Do you feel guilty because you find yourself rooting against the person?

Here's how to score your answers:

12 = low maintenance: a person who's worth keeping in your life.

13-24 = medium maintenance: is this relationship really worth your time?

25-36 = high maintenance: leave (if you can) before this person sucks the life out of you.

If you're in a relationship with a pathologically needy person, the obvious answer is to get out. But if the relationship matters to you and you still want to save it, one option is to give the person the chance to reform.

Derrick, for example, loved it at first when his girlfriend Jada sought his opinions about her job, her life, and even her clothes. But finally it dawned on him that her neediness never ended, and he grew tired of her failure to take responsibility for her own life, her ceaseless meltdowns and emotional requests for help, and her chronic whining.

Derrick came to me looking for a solution, and I advised him to use an approach I call the "wince confrontation." I told him to say the following to Jada, while making it clear that it pained him to say it:

"I'm getting close to avoiding you, because almost every time I ask you about something you haven't done you make an excuse or blame someone else. And almost every time I confront you about ways in which you need to improve, you either act hurt, start to cry, or get angry. All of us feel disappointed, hurt, or upset from time to time, but if you get angry or emotional each time, it's too exhausting to be around. You have the right to react in any way you choose, but I have the right to excuse myself or avoid you—which is what I will do And that's not going to help our relationship. So I hope you'll start taking responsibility for yourself, and find a way to keep from falling apart when you're feeling upset."

A situation like this can go one of two ways. If the person is smart enough to take your message seriously, you'll see a change for the better. On the other hand, the person may refuse to change, or even escalate the needy behavior, in which case you may decide that the relationship isn't worth saving after all.

This may seem like pretty strong medicine, and it's not something you should have to say to other people. With needy people, however, you need strong medicine. Being needy is an action, and the dictum "words respond to words, but actions respond to counteractions" is doubly true when you're dealing with this toxic behavior.

If you're coping with a needy person, one warning is in order: Extreme and highly pathological neediness can sometimes be a sign of borderline personality disorder. People with this disorder also exhibit these behaviors:

■ They demand more than they whine.

■ They desperately fear abandonment.

■ They cycle between idealizing you ("You're my reason for living") and devaluing you ("You're selfish, just like everybody else").

■ They have no core personality. They seem empty because they *are* empty, and to fill that hole they parasitically latch on to whoever is closest.

■ They act impulsively. For instance, they seek out unsafe sex or drive far too fast.

■ They have extreme mood swings, often have angry outbursts, and may threaten suicide.

■ They may act paranoid ("You act like you care but you're just out to hurt me").

If you're dealing with a person who acts this way, you're in trouble. Your safest option, if you're not in too deep at this stage and the relationship isn't important to you, is to escape—but carefully, because people with borderline personality disorder can become stalkers.

Borderline personality disorder is treatable, but even professionals find it tough to help these people. Try to rescue a person with borderline personality on your own, and you'll go down in flames together.

■ Bullies

In my line of work, I encounter bullied people all the time, but people hardly ever try to bully me personally. The last occasion, however, was pretty memorable.

I was at the murder trial of O. J. Simpson, watching the proceedings at the prosecution's request. The lawyers wanted me to offer suggestions (which they didn't heed often enough . . . but that's a different story).

Suddenly, at one point in the trial, the infamous defense attorney F. Lee Bailey asked Mark Fuhrman—the investigating officer under attack by the defense at the time—if he knew me. Pointing me out in the courtroom, Bailey falsely insinuated that I'd coached Fuhrman on his testimony. Instantly, I found myself in the spotlight, and on national TV.

Later, in a meeting with the prosecution lawyers and me, Bailey tried to make this same accusation to my face. But I know something about handling people like Bailey, so I didn't do what he expected.

For several minutes, Bailey said things like, "Dr. Goulston we don't know exactly why you're here, but we know you've been here through most of the trial." As he talked, I just looked him squarely in the eye. Instead of saying or doing anything, I simply blinked occasionally.

Finally another attorney looked at me and said, "Mark, you haven't said anything." At that point I said, "He hasn't asked me a question." I went right back to looking Bailey in the eye, and he flinched slightly.

Next Bailey asked if I'd brainwashed or drugged Fuhrman or somehow done something to prepare him for his testimony. I was reminded of when he'd cornered Fuhrman during the cross examination, in the unforgettable "N-word" incident. Clearly, Bailey was hoping I'd panic and say something stupid he could twist or distort.

Even when you're innocent, it's pretty intimidating to be grilled by F. Lee Bailey. However, I had the advantage of seeing through his game: His goal was to disarm, frustrate, and then outrage me, so I'd lose my cool.

So when he asked if I'd drugged or brainwashed Fuhrman—an outrageous question—I waited for a full count of seven and then cleared my throat. At that point everyone in the room was waiting breathlessly to hear what I'd say. I counted to another full count of seven, and said to Bailey, "Excuse me Mr. Bailey, my mind wandered over the past few minutes. Can you please repeat what you said?"

He was absolutely dumbfounded. How could I dare find the world's most intimidating lawyer so boring as to become distracted? And after that he backed down—proving that if you don't play a bully's game, he usually doesn't have a backup plan.

The lesson is simple: Bullies come after you because they think you're easy prey. Refuse to follow their script, and they'll usually give up and seek an easier target.

Sometimes, of course, there's no good way to stand up to a bully. For instance, if you desperately need your current job and your boss has the power to hire and fire on a whim, your only real options may be to lay low, minimize contact with the person, and look for a less toxic work environment. Even in this case, however, you'll be a less desirable target if you stop looking vulnerable.

When a bully tries to intimidate you by verbally attacking you, do this. Make eye contact. Act perfectly polite but ever-so-slightly bored, as if your mind is elsewhere. Let your body language transmit the same message: Stand up straight, be relaxed, and cock your head as if you're listening but not very hard. Let your arms hang casually, instead of folding them defensively across your chest. Often, this response makes bullies feel uncomfortable or even foolish and causes them to back down.

If you're in a position where you can take some risks, you have additional options when it comes to handling bullies. My favorite approach, which catches most bullies completely off-guard, is to strike back—hard. Bullies act the way they do because they get away with it, but deep down most of them know it's not an ideal strategy. Sometimes they just need someone to say that to their face.

"The one thing I'm most happy about right now is that I don't work for you," I said emphatically.

"What?" replied my dinner companion in surprise. I'd just met Frank, a 43-year-old Senior V.P. of Sales at a rapidly growing company, and already he'd made a condescending, sexually demeaning comment to our waitress at the famed Polo Lounge of the Beverly Hills Hotel. Our waitress could only smile back at him uncomfortably and then glance at me, as if to ask "Who's your creepy friend?"

I looked Frank in the eye. "Yeah, I wouldn't want to work for you because I'd be deathly afraid to tell you if I made a mistake. That's because you have a capacity for disdain that crosses over into abuse. Life is just too short to put up with crap from a bully like you."

His jaw dropped. Looking at me incredulously, he said, "Nobody's ever talked to me that way."

"Well," I said, since I was indeed bullying him at the time, "maybe it takes one to know one. But more importantly, is it true?"

"It's all true. It cost me a marriage, a relationship with my kids, and a job," Frank confessed. Then he leaned forward and, as if he didn't want anyone to hear, whispered, "Is it curable?"

I replied, without missing a beat: "It's an addiction. The best you can be is a bully in recovery. You have to work on it every day or else you'll slide back. But it's probably worth it, because at the end of your life you'll be less bitter and have more friends, and people won't have to lie at your funeral to come up with nice things to say about you. You'll accomplish more than you thought possible."

He laughed. "Can you help me?"

I pondered that for a moment. "I'm trying to figure out whether you're a bully to your core. If you delight in beating up on people, especially those who can't fight back, like our waitress here, then I won't help you," I said. "That's because you've already taken from life more than you deserve. Furthermore, I would help anyone you bullied to beat you. If, however, you act like a bully because it gets things done and you don't know any better, then there is some wiggle room. I might work with you."

On that note, I paused to see what he'd do. And he gave me the job.

Like this guy, many bullies are so accustomed to their victims prostrating themselves and cowering—and so contemptuous when this happens—that they're knocked for a loop when someone bullies them back. It's a high-risk move, but the payoff can be big. However, try this approach only if you don't mind losing a client or a contract and make sure you have an exit strategy.

■ TAKERS

You know these people. They're the ones who hit you up every day for a favor ("Could you cover the phones for me?" "Take my kids to soccer practice?" "Pick up the lunch tab?"). Strangely, however, they never seem to have time or energy to help you in return.

These people usually won't ruin your life, but they can ruin your day. They can make you look unproductive (because you're doing their work instead of your own), cause you to feel resentful, and take time away from the things you want to be doing.

Avoid takers when you can, but if that's not possible, neutralize them. How? It's the easiest trick in the book. The next time a taker asks you for a favor, follow this scenario.

> TAKER: Hey, could you do the graphs for my PowerPoint presentation? I know I should do them, but I'm swamped.
>
> YOU: Sure. No problem! And you can help me out by taking over the intern orientation on Thursday.
>
> TAKER: Uhhhh. . . .
>
> YOU: I assume you don't mind doing a favor for me in return, right?
>
> TAKER: Uhhh. . . .

Do this once or twice—and do *insist* each time on a quid pro quo—and the taker will move on to an easier touch. Also, identify takers ahead of time and always have a request ready to ask of them. It's a great approach because you don't say "no" or get mad or give the person any reason to take offense. Thus, you don't create an enemy; you simply send the person off in search of another patsy.

■ NARCISSISTS

These people aren't out to hurt you, but they don't give a damn about you either—except as an audience for their own wonderfulness. Narcissists don't mirror your feelings and emotions, because they're too busy saying: "Mirror, mirror on the wall—who's the fairest of them all?" and answering themselves, "I am!" A friend of mine, Edward Hollander, calls them "mental masturbators" because they really just want to stroke themselves.

A narcissist's motto is, "So . . . enough about you." (And that's true even if you haven't opened your mouth yet!) Narcissists are always on center stage, expecting you to sit in the wings and clap for them. They'll interrupt your stories, ignore your successes while trumpeting theirs, and expect you to treat their problems as vastly more serious than what they see as your own petty issues.

However, narcissists (unlike the psychopaths I discuss later) aren't necessarily bad people at heart. Often, they're just spoiled. Sometimes they're even okay to work with, if you understand their behavior. For instance, if your business partner is a narcissist, manage your expectations by never expecting the person to do something that is not in his or her best interest. That way you won't feel blindsided when the person acts narcissistically, and you'll be able to keep your wits about you.

How can you tell if you're dealing with a narcissist? Do this "narcissist inventory," rating the person on a 1-to-3 scale (1 = rarely; 2 = sometimes; 3 = frequently):

- How often does the person need to be right at all costs?
- How often does the person act impatient with you for no good reason?
- How often does the person interrupt you in the middle of what you're saying, and yet take offense if you interrupt?

- How often does the person expect you to drop whatever you're thinking about and listen to him or her—and does the person take offense when you expect the same in return?
- How often does the person talk more than he or she listens?
- How often does the person say "Yes, but," "That's not true," "No," "However," or "Your problem is"?
- How often does the person resist and resent doing something that matters to you, just because it's inconvenient?
- How often does the person expect you to cheerfully do something that's inconvenient for you?
- How often does the person expect you to accept behavior that he or she would refuse to accept from you?
- How often does the person fail to say "Thank You," "I'm sorry," "Congratulations," or "Excuse me" when it's called for?

To score your inventory, add up the total:
10-16 = The person is cooperative
17-23 = The person is argumentative
24-30 = The person is a narcissist

If you can't change a narcissist, should you reach out or back away? It depends, because narcissists can be exciting partners in a personal or business relationship. Nearly all politicians are narcissists (who else would put their families through all that?). So are most actors, and many hard-driving lawyers and CEOs.

Narcissists often are huge successes in life, and going along for the ride can be a heady experience. Sometimes, it'll get you to high places. Other times, it'll humiliate you (as Eliot Spitzer's wife learned when he tumbled from grace). It's your call—but don't expect a fifty-fifty relationship if you stay.

■ PSYCHOPATHS

Years ago, researcher Robert Hare sent a paper to a scientific journal and got back a very odd reply. The paper, by Hare and his graduate students, contained photos of electroencephalographs (EEGs—brain wave tracings) of adult men performing a simple language task. The editor rejected the paper outright, saying that the EEGs "couldn't have come from real people."

In a way, the journal editor was right. The brain scans were from psychopaths: cold-blooded, ruthless people who seem to lack some key piece of what makes us human. These people are different from the rest of us biologically, and they're different emotionally as well.

About one in every hundred people is a psychopath, and most of these people aren't behind bars. In fact, the core traits of a classic psychopath—coldness, lack of empathy, self-centeredness, ruthlessness—make them some of the world's most financially successful business leaders. The not-so-bright ones wind up in prison, but the smarter ones often wind up as CEOs. They're also sexually driven and superficially charming, so plenty of them populate the dating scene. Most of them are men, but some of the most cold-blooded are women.

Odds are, you'll run into one of these people at some point in your life. If so, follow this rule: get away. Go. Run. Chew off your leg to escape the trap, if you have to. Because these people will ruin you financially, crush you emotionally, and destroy your life if it helps them—and they'll never look back.

Most people make the mistake of trying to reason with a psychopath or touch the person's heartstrings. But you cannot touch these people emotionally. You cannot win them over, make them feel sorry for you, or make them want to help you in any way. They may pretend to care about you (in fact, they're extraordinarily good at conning people emotionally) but they don't. Instead, they're masters of the "bait and switch." They bait you by knowing how to tap into your dreams and your fears. This lessens the mirror neuron gap between you and them and causes you to trust and believe them. Then, when they have you hooked, they use you to get what they want.

How can you spot a psychopath? It's harder than you'd think, but here are clues: They manipulate people like chess pieces, with no regard to the pain they cause. They're predatory thrill seekers. They lie easily and don't care if they get caught. They're glib, charismatic, and charming. They crave power and do whatever it takes to get it. They use people for sexual or financial purposes and then discard them.

Again, do not make the mistake of thinking that you can "handle" these people. I make a living getting through to people, and I'm extremely good at it—but none of the approaches I teach in this book will work with a psychopath. Quite simply, these people lack the neural mechanisms to respond to you in a reciprocal moral or ethical way. Think of a psychopath as an exotic but deadly animal—say, a scorpion—and steer clear. Do this even if you lose money or a promotion or a job. No matter what the cost, you'll pay a far higher price if you stay connected.

■ Mirror Check: Who's the Problem?

The people I've talked about here are some of the toxic people you'll encounter in life. There are plenty of others, but most of them are easy to reach and easy to change (and even easier to avoid, if you're smart). In the chapters that follow, you'll find methods for neutralizing them, getting rid of them, or even turning them into assets.

However, when you encounter toxic people and attempt to analyze their problems, always keep one thing in mind. Is it possible—just barely possible—that the person with the problem is *you?*

For instance, if you're a guy who thinks every girl you date is nuts, you may need to look in the mirror for the source of the problem. On one hand, you may be attracted to screwed-up females with whom you can have only unhappy relationships. On the other hand, you may be attributing your own personal problems to your girlfriends. Maybe they seem hysterical because you really do tend to ignore them, dependent and whiny because you've made promises that you haven't followed through on, paranoid because you're dishonest or evasive, or borderline because you're alternately controlling and abandoning. (How can you tell? The best way to know for sure is if all these so-called crazy women are happily married or in long-term relationships a few years down the road. If so, that's a pretty big clue.)

When you take that hard look in the mirror, it's possible you'll realize that you're the one who's a little nuts. But not to worry. We all screw up in different ways, and what separates the good people from the toxic ones is the ability to face those screw-ups and learn a lesson from them. Take it from one who knows.

> I was driving home in a rage. Seven minutes earlier, my wife had crossed over the line. She'd interrupted me in the middle of a psychotherapy session with a very disturbed patient. In such meetings, my concentration tended to be intense. I had warned her on several occasions not to call me at these times. (Apparently in those days you could get me to listen only if you paid me.)
>
> I picked up the receiver and could tell it was her and I said, "*What?*" (as in "What the hell are you doing calling me?"). I sensed what I felt was inconsideration at interrupting me in her voice.
>
> The next second, however, she said, "Please don't be angry at me!" in a pleading voice. "I'm lying on the bathroom floor and I can't move," she continued. Instantly I knew she had much bigger things on her mind than being fearful of my reaction. She was terrified.
>
> "I'm leaving now!" I told her in a firm, take-charge voice. I apologized to my patient, saying that a family emergency had occurred and we would need to continue our session at another time. I got into my car, called 911, and was put on hold.
>
> As I drove, the frustration I felt toward the emergency operator was a thin veneer over the fury I felt at myself—how could I be such a hypocrite?—for apparently communicating to my wife that she couldn't call me in a situation like this. And both of these overlay my own fear of what might be happening.
>
> When I arrived home I ran upstairs to the bathroom where my wife said to me, "Thank you for coming home, please don't be angry at me."
>
> To my estimate, I had never and have never been abusive, but the firm boundary I'd set with regard to calling me during work clearly crossed over into either abuse or at least a huge failure in my role as protector to the people I love.
>
> "Don't worry, it will be okay, and DON'T apologize," I said, wondering what kind of self-centered, piece-of-crap husband I was to have put my wife in the position of being scared to call me when she was afraid for her life.

By the way, it turned out to be a ruptured ovarian cyst and everything worked out fine. But I realized at that moment that my wife and children should at least have the privilege I gave my patients to interrupt me anytime, anywhere if they were in a scary situation.

Had I acted stupidly in denying them that privilege? Yes. Was my behavior toxic? Yes.

But like I said—we all screw up. The key, if you catch yourself being toxic, is to ensure that you never make the same mistake in the future. In my case, the message was plain: Physician, heal thyself.

➡ *Usable Insight*

If you're hesitant to say "No," you may be neurotic. If you're truly afraid to say "No," you're probably dealing with a toxic person. And if nobody ever says "No" to you, that toxic person could be you.

➡ *Action Step*

Make a list of the people who play a key role in your life. Beside each name, answer these questions: Can I count on this person to provide me with practical assistance? Emotional support? Financial support? Prompt and willing help when I'm in trouble? Wherever you see lots of "no" answers, think about expecting more from that person—or about easing the person out of your life.

Now, for the hard part: Make a list of the people who count on *you* and answer these same questions: Do you provide these people with practical assistance? Emotional support? Financial support? Prompt and willing help when they're in trouble? If you're honest, you'll probably spot some answers that make you cringe. If so, take the steps you need to take to be a positive person—not a toxic one.

12 Easy-to-Use Tools for Achieving Buy-in and Getting Through

Now that you know the core rules for reaching people, you're ready to arm yourself with some powerful tools for moving people through the Persuasion Cycle.

The following techniques take just minutes, but they can change the course of a business project, a sale, a relationship, or even a life. Add them to your communication arsenal and you'll get through to people you never thought you could reach.

I've identified the key points in the Persuasion Cycle where each intervention is often most effective, but they're highly flexible—so use them anytime, in any situation, when your goal is to persuade someone to do the "impossible."

12

THE IMPOSSIBILITY QUESTION

Benefit: Move a person from listening to considering—and from "Yes . . . but" to "Yes!"

Most of the things worth doing in the world had been declared impossible before they were done.
—LOUIS D. BRANDEIS,
20TH-CENTURY SUPREME COURT JUSTICE

B irds fly, but people can't. You can't record music. You can't market a Pet Rock. And you certainly can't become a multimillionaire by selling books online.

Why? Because everybody says so . . . or at least everybody used to. Of course, that was before somebody did each of these things.

If you're that somebody—the Wilbur Wright, Thomas Edison, Gary Dahl, or Jeff Bezos who's trying to transform a vision into reality—your biggest problem isn't realizing that your goal is possible. It's talking other people into seeing that it's possible. It's getting your coworkers, your clients, your employees, your boss, your investors, or your family to go from "we can't do it" to "maybe we can do it" to "let's do it."

Years ago, Dave Hibbard, the co-founder of Dialexis, taught me one of the most powerful tricks for turning a situation around if you're being held hostage by people who can't get past "can't." He calls it the Impossibility Question, but I like to call it "kicking but."

The Impossibility Question works with a person who's some-where between resisting and listening, but not ready to move to considering. Typically, the person is wavering between fear ("this is a threatening idea, and it will fail and ruin me") and apathy ("this may be a good idea, but it sounds like too much effort on my part"). If you're lucky, there might be a flicker of interest in there some-where ("Hmmm . . . could it work? Who knows?"). But without a shove, your idea is going nowhere. That powerful shove is the Impossibility Question.

Here's how it works.

> **You:** What's something that would be impossible to do, but if you could do it, would dramatically increase your success?
>
> **Other person:** If I could just do ____ , but that's impossible.
>
> **You:** Okay. What would make it possible?

That's it, just two quick questions: "What's something that would be impossible?" and, "What would make it possible?"

What's so powerful about those two questions? They move a per-son from a defensive, closed position or a selfish, excuse-making stance into an open, thinking attitude. And they make the person picture your vision as a reality and cooperate in thinking strategi-cally about reaching that reality.

When you ask people to tell you something that's impossible, you are in essence getting them to say something positive: "I believe this is impossible." Thinking and saying that shifts their minds into a positive (agreeing) movement toward you. Once they're in that "Yes" vs. "No" or "Yes, but" mode and you agree with them but add the twist—"What would make it possible?"—they're poised to cooperate.

This approach is a little like the martial arts ploy that uses an opponent's offensive move against the person by pulling the oppo-nent off balance instead of striking back. It works because rather than resisting that movement you mirror it and invite it, causing the other person to go off balance. Once this happens, the person moves from resisting or thinking to considering, and you have traction.

That doesn't mean the person will buy in instantly. Sometimes, the first reply will be snarky or hostile: "Well, give me a million bucks and a staff of 80 people and that deadline would be possible." But wait quietly, and the person's mind will take hold of the question you posed and feel compelled to give you an answer. In effect, you've created a mental itch that needs to be scratched, and the only way to scratch it is by answering the question. When you get that answer, you're in.

Several years ago, I used the Impossibility Question with a segment producer on the television show *The View*. He'd done a capable and competent job of preparing me for a segment in which I was the guest expert, and we got to talking about his dream of being an executive producer. He was smart and creative and talented, but I could see he was still stuck in "can't"—as in, "I can't do what I want because there's too much competition and it's a cutthroat business and I don't have the edge I need."

So I asked him: "What is something that would be impossible, but if you could do it would rapidly accelerate your career wish to become an executive producer?"

He was hesitant at first, but then he responded with: "If I could find out where Chandra Levy is" (this was before she was discovered dead in Washington, D.C.) "and arrange an exclusive interview with Barbara Walters, that would put me on the radar screen and greatly help my progress toward doing what I want to do."

I replied: "So even if you don't do that, if you can arrange for an exclusive interview by Barbara with a highly sought-after guest, you could accomplish the same thing. Correct?"

"Correct," he replied and as he was about to leave the green room he stopped, turned back to me and said: "I've been doing this kind of work for over 10 years and *never* has a guest asked me such a helpful question. Thanks." Without planning it, I'd succeeded in also accomplishing the impossible for myself—that is, becoming memorable to a producer who must deal with hundreds of guests like me in a year.

How can you use the Impossibility Question in your own life? The power of this question lies in its flexibility: it works in any sit-

on, business or personal, where improvement is vital but peo-
say "It can't be done." Here are two quick examples.

#1: THE IMPOSSIBILITY QUESTION IN SALES

SALES MANAGER: What's something that would be impossible to do, but if you could do it, it would dramatically increase your sales?

SALESPERSON: If I could get Company X to try our payroll management system, which is much better than the one they're using now, it would get us to a new level of clients.

SALES MANAGER: Okay, what would make that possible?

SALESPERSON: What if our CEO found a way to speak to the CEO of Company X, since the two of them are pretty equal in stature? And, hey . . . maybe our marketing person could figure out a way to invite a few CEOs of other companies to a meeting—maybe something fun that our CEO and company could host.

SALES MANAGER: Hmm, not a bad idea. It wouldn't be easy to do, but it's not impossible.

#2: THE IMPOSSIBILITY QUESTION IN CUSTOMER SERVICE

SENIOR MANAGER OF A CUSTOMER SERVICE DEPARTMENT FOR A COMPANY THAT SELLS BUSINESS SOFTWARE: What would be impossible to do, but if we could do it, it would dramatically increase our customer's satisfaction with our products?

CUSTOMER SERVICE TEAM MEMBER: To be able to read our customers' minds and predict who's going to be a pain in the rear after they buy a product, because they're the ones who tend to badmouth us to everyone they know.

SENIOR MANAGER: What would make that possible?

TEAM MEMBER: What about asking customers when they buy one of our products if we can call them a week later to check with them on how the product is working for them and to walk them through additional tips on how to get even more out of it? That way we can find out who's having problems, and get them back on track.

SENIOR MANAGER: Great. Let's do it.

It's that simple, and it works in any dynamic: coworker to co-worker, boss to employee, even employee to boss. But don't keep the Impossibility Question locked in your drawer at work, because it's a hell of a tool for changing things at home, too.

For instance, ask your partner, "What would make it possible for us to spend more time with our kids and put in less overtime and still be okay financially?" Or ask a teenager, "What would make it possible for you to be safe and still be able to do many of the things you really want to do?" Or ask an aging parent who's living with you, "What would make it possible for you to feel less unhappy about giving up driving?"

When you do this, the people you connect with will solve problems you thought were unsolvable. In fact, they'll stop being the problem, and start being the solution—and the possibilities will be endless.

➡ **Usable Insight**
Invite people to tell you what they think is impossible, and they'll lower their guard to consider what's possible.

➡ **Action Step**
Ask someone at home or work to name an impossible goal the person would like to accomplish or achieve. Respond with, "I agree with you. That sounds impossible, so what would make it possible?" Then help the person brainstorm the steps to turn the goal into a reality.

13

THE MAGIC PARADOX

Benefit: Shift another person from resistance to listening—from "nobody understands" to "you understand."

Do the unexpected. The expected is boring.
The expected is tuned out.
—STEVE STRAUSS, AUTHOR, *THE SMALL BUSINESS BIBLE*

Most magic is sleight of hand, but the Magic Paradox is sleight of mind. When you act as if your goal is the exact opposite of what you're trying to accomplish, that's the Magic Paradox—and as the name implies, it's powerful magic.

This technique lets you break through to people in the most difficult part of the communication cycle: at the very beginning, when you need to shift them from resisting to listening and then to considering. It's a classic first step in hostage negotiation, and it's equally powerful in a business crisis.

To see how the Magic Paradox works, picture this scenario. You're Art's manager and he's not producing. You know he's going through a divorce, and you're cutting him as much slack as you can, but now he's imploding and your project is in danger as a result. You don't want to fire Art because you know he can do the job and there's no time to train anyone else. But you need to light a fire under him somehow, or everybody's in trouble.

Here's what you *don't* do if you're smart. You don't go to Art and say something like, "Look, I know things are tough but you need to get your act together. You know how to do this job, and I know you can pull it off. Just set some targets, and I'm sure you can get caught up in time. All of us are under pressure, and we're counting on you."

If you do this (as most managers would), odds are Art will get defensive and hit back with "Yes . . . but." As in, "Yes . . . but there's not enough time." Or, "Yes . . . but nobody's giving me any support." Keep pushing, and he'll back further into defensiveness and lash out angrily or even quit.

That's not what you need. And it's not what Art needs. So instead, do what Art least expects: Empathize with his negative thoughts.

For example, say: "I'll bet you feel that nobody knows what it's like to be scared that you can't pull this project off. And I'll bet that you're upset because you think we're all feeling let down by you. What's more, I'll bet you feel that nobody can possibly understand how hard it is to deal with all the stuff that's happening in your life."

Now watch the magic. Because you're empathizing with Art's emotions, you will eliminate his mirror neuron gap and cause him to feel understood by and connected to you. And there's the first paradox: By saying explicitly that you know he feels that nobody understands, you'll make him realize that you *do* understand.

Here's the second paradox: When you spell out all of Art's reasons for being negative, you'll shift him into a more positive attitude. Initially he'll probably rise to ambivalence, that in-between place where he says, "Yeah, it's godawful right now. But I know you need me to do this, and I'll see if I can pull it off. Just don't expect miracles." At that point, you'll have enough forward momentum to nudge him to make the leap all the way to acceptance: "I know I've screwed up. But I can do this. I really can. If you just give me a few days, I can make up for lost time."

▪ THE CASCADE OF "YES"

How does the Magic Paradox work? By setting into motion a cascade of "yes" coming from the other person ("Yes, you're right, my life is a mess, and I can't take it anymore"), you shift the person's attitude from disagreement to agreement. Once you establish that rapport, the person is emotionally primed to cooperate instead of punch back. Remember back to the hostage scenario in Chapter 1, and you'll recognize that this is the same approach Detective Kramer used to defuse a potentially deadly situation.

Like Kramer, I've used the Magic Paradox to create instant attitude shifts in life-and-death situations. At one point in my career, for instance, I treated a deeply depressed woman who'd tried to commit suicide twice after being the victim of a brutal rape. She sat across from me for six months, saying very little and never making eye contact. Then one day, as she talked about the many terrible things she'd suffered in her life, I experienced my own emotional shift and suddenly felt the full weight of her lifetime of despair descend on me. The overwhelming grayness I felt sucked the colors out of the room, and I could hardly breathe.

Without even thinking, I blurted out, "I never knew it was so bad. And I can't help you kill yourself, but if you do, I will still think well of you. I'll miss you, and maybe I'll understand why you needed to." I was horrified as soon as I said it—I'd actually given my patient permission to kill herself! But as my words hung in the air between us, the woman turned to me and made full eye contact with me for the first time in our relationship. And then she smiled, and simply said: "If you can really understand why I might need to kill myself, maybe I won't have to." And she didn't. In fact, she married, had children, and became a psychologist. And she led me to discover the power of the Magic Paradox.

Similarly, you can use this technique at work or at home in a very tense situation when you need to keep another person from making a serious mistake. Here's an example involving Rose and her teenage daughter Lizzie, who's hanging out with a guy Mom knows is a bad influence.

> LIZZIE (IN A LOUD, ANGRY VOICE): That's it! I've had it with you and all your rules! I'm moving in with Ryan, and I'm 18 now so you can't stop me.

ROSE (TAKING A DEEP BREATH AND RESISTING THE URGE TO YELL IN RESPONSE): Let's talk for just a minute. You know, I'll bet you feel that nobody knows what it's like to feel suffocated by the rules we ask you to follow.

LIZZIE: That's right! I do feel suffocated!

ROSE: And I'll bet that you're angry because you think we can't understand how hard it is for you right now to be nearly grown-up and still have to live with your parents.

LIZZIE (STARTING TO CALM DOWN): Yeah.

ROSE: What's more, I'll bet you feel that we don't have any idea the kind of pressure you're under, or the really tough decisions you're trying to make in your life.

LIZZIE (EXHALING): They *are* tough. And I can't talk to you about them, because you and Dad have your own problems, especially now that he's been laid off.

ROSE: It is hard right now, but your problems are every bit as important as ours. In fact, maybe if we sit down and talk about everything that's going on, we'll both feel better. Do you have a few minutes to share a cup of tea with your mom?

LIZZIE: Okay, sure.

At the beginning of this conversation, Lizzie sees Rose as the enemy. But by using the Magic Paradox, Mom creates a cascade of "yes" that ratchets Lizzie's emotional level down to the degree at which she's willing to declare a truce. In short, Lizzie's gone from resistance to listening to considering, all in the span of just a few sentences—and as a result, Mom has a much better shot at talking her out of a big life mistake.

■ A TRUST-GAINING MOVE

The Magic Paradox isn't just a tool for helping someone exhale or convincing a person to make the right move instead of the wrong one. It's also a strong hand to play if you need to gain the trust and confidence of a person who's not in a trusting frame of mind, and it's a power move if you're working in a toxic environment and want another person to know that you're not part of the problem.

> Jack was the new managing partner of a law firm in Los Angeles. The firm wanted to build up its staff of female associates, but it had a reputation for working them to death and creating tremendous stress—especially in those female associates who had young kids. These associates always felt guilty about pawning their kids off on hired help and spending too little time with them.
>
> One day Shannon, a third-year associate, was having a meltdown because her three-year-old child had told her for the umpteenth time, "I hate that you have to go to work, and I don't like you anymore." The incident pushed Shannon over the edge, and she sat with her head on her desk crying when Jack walked by and saw her through a crack in her door.
>
> The prior managing partner just ignored such scenes, but Jack felt differently because he too loved his kids and felt grateful that his wife was able to stay home with them. He was taking steps to make his firm more family friendly, but he knew it would take time and he knew how frustrated the younger moms were.
>
> Jack knocked on the door and politely said, "Hey Shannon, mind if I come in?"
>
> Shannon picked her head up and said, "No it's alright, I'll be okay."
>
> Jack knew that Shannon would pull herself together, but he was bothered that the firm claimed to be female friendly, but did not carry through on its promise. He stepped in her office and closed the door behind him.
>
> He looked at her and said, "Shannon, I'll bet you feel that there is almost never a time when you aren't letting someone down. If it's not your child, it's the office; if it's not the office, it's your child. Isn't that true?"
>
> Shannon looked up at him, paused, and then burst into tears and said, "I just hate upsetting my kid and not being able to do what the partners want of me, and I hate that I've started smoking again and I've gained 20 pounds."
>
> She stopped, slightly alarmed that she'd voiced these private thoughts to a colleague. Then Jack added: "And I'll bet you feel it's getting worse instead of better, isn't that true also?"

Shannon started crying harder. Jack didn't try to stop her, because he knew she needed to vent her anger and frustration. The only thing he said was: "It really is hard being an associate and a mom."

Shannon merely said, "Uh-huh," but within a few minutes her tears began to lessen. As her storm of tears passed, so did the worst of her feelings of failure and helplessness. After a moment, she stood up from her desk, walked over to Jack, and gave him a hug and said, "Thanks, you're a good boss and a good guy." Jack smiled with embarrassment and replied: "You're a good lawyer *and* a good mom!"

Up to then, Shannon saw Jack as part of the problem at her firm: just another guy who expected the impossible and didn't care about collateral damage. By the time he left her office, she saw him in a completely different light: as a supportive colleague who respected her and deserved her respect and best efforts in return.

Jack accomplished this transformation—one that altered his entire relationship with his colleague for years to come—in less time than it takes some managers to order lunch. How did he do it? By understanding the secret of the Magic Paradox: If you want people to do the unexpected, you go first.

➡ *Usable Insight*
When you start a conversation by saying "No" for another person, it opens the door for that person to say "Yes."

➡ *Action Step*
Select someone at work who's resistant to cooperating with you and either makes excuses for not doing something or responds with a "Yes, but." (Be sure the person is actually capable of doing the job and has enough time and resources to accomplish it.)

1. Say to the person: "I'll bet you feel that there is no way you're going to be able to do what it is that I'm asking you to do, isn't that true?" If you're on track the person will nod, and be puzzled and slightly disarmed by your understanding.

2. Follow that with: "And I'll bet you're hesitant to tell me straight out that you can't get it done, isn't *that* also true?" The person will probably nod in agreement or even say, "Yes" in response.

3. Finally say, "In fact you may be thinking that the only way to get that done would be to do _____." (Let the person fill in the blank.)

4. Then work with the person to make that solution a reality.

14

THE EMPATHY JOLT

*Benefit: Transition a person from resisting
to "willing to do" in a single step,
by changing the dynamics of a relationship.*

Great anger is more destructive than the sword.
—INDIAN PROVERB

E arly in my career, I grew tired of listening to coworkers, couples, and family members who refused to listen to each other. I hated the "he said/she said" wars. I hated the zero-sum games. In these infantile debates, the best I could achieve was a temporary truce. More often, I felt like I was putting a temporary bandage on a gaping, hemorrhaging wound.

I had a name for the culprits in these situations: "ignorant blamers." These were the people who treated communication as a blood sport, ranting relentlessly about another person's failings without giving a second's thought to how the attacked party felt. ("And Bob always lets his projects run over the time we've budgeted. And he never listens to my suggestions because he thinks he knows everything. And he acts like he's so high and mighty. And nobody likes him because he's not a team player. And here's another thing. . . .")

The ignorant blamers were, above all, presumptuous: They presumed to tell both me and the other person what the score was.

They weren't the least bit curious about what their partners, co-workers, or children thought. In the mind of ignorant blamers, the goal wasn't to share information but to expose every flaw of the other person, sit back, and say, "So—what are you going to do about it?"

Attempting to calm such people down or get them to listen to others rarely was effective. Then one day I spontaneously happened upon an intervention that changed everything.

It happened when the Franklin family came in to see me because their 15-year-old son, Harry, was refusing to do his home-work, help around the house, or cooperate in almost any way. Time-outs, taking away the Internet, or sending him to his room had little to no effect and only caused him to become even more sullen. His mother, Joan, appeared to be much more upset about the situation than his father, Robert.

As soon as the three of them sat down in my office, I asked why they'd come to see me. Joan launched into a list of complaints about Harry. Robert sat quietly in a way that communicated that he agreed with Joan's complaints, but also understood how Harry could be so ticked off at how she went on and on about them. Meanwhile, Harry sat with his arms crossed and his baseball cap pulled down over his face, signaling that the last place he wanted to be at this moment was in this room.

I had to find a way to engage Harry and also Robert without alienating Joan. So I tried something new.

"Joan," I said firmly and assertively, without any hostility or frus-tration in my voice, "if I were to ask Harry why he thinks this meet-ing is just going to be a waste of time and money, what would he say?"

"What?" Joan replied, with her laundry list of complaints against Harry not yet expressed.

I repeated the question, adding, "Joan, please put yourself in Harry's shoes and tell me why he thinks this meeting is a waste of time and won't accomplish anything."

At that point, several interesting things happened. Joan paused, Robert gave me a puzzled but curious look, and behatted son Harry loosened his crossed arms and lifted his chin off his chest ever so slightly, indicating that I'd caught his interest.

Joan thought for a moment and replied, "He'd probably say this is going to be a waste of time because all that's going to happen is that Mom's going to lecture me and Dad's going to just go along with it and probably not say anything. And that's just what happens at home."

"Really?" I said, to emphasize the significance of Joan's shift from attacking to understanding. Then I added: "And if I were to ask Harry how frustrated that makes him feel, what would he say?"

Joan replied, "He'd say he can't stand it."

"And if I were to ask him what he does or wants to do as a result, what would he say to that?" I added.

"He'd say he wants to tune it all out and try to get away as soon as possible," Joan replied.

By this time both Harry and Robert were riveted on this dialogue between Joan and me.

I turned to Robert and said: "Robert, if I were to ask what frustrates Joan most about how you deal with the situation with Harry, what would she say?"

At this point, Joan and even Harry became interested in what Robert would say.

Robert paused and then replied, "Joan would probably say I sabotage her by agreeing on the surface with her but communicating to Harry that I agree with him about how over the top she can get."

"And if I asked Joan how that made her feel, what would she say?" I asked.

Robert said: "All alone, with everyone fighting her and nobody helping her."

At that point Joan began to cry and said, "I hate being such a bitch, but life is about details and if everybody ignores them Harry is going to fall through the cracks."

At this point, I could finally make out Harry's eyes under the hat, and he'd uncrossed his arms. I asked him, "Harry, if I were to ask your mom and dad whether they're more disappointed and frustrated with you or worried about you, what would they say?"

Harry hesitated and then replied with a sense of revelation, "I guess they'd both say they were worried about me."

"And what would they say they were worried about?" I asked.

"That I'd turn out to be a loser and have a shitty life . . . but they're so frickin controlling I can't breathe," he replied.

"I know their style sucks, but stay with the first thing you said. Why would they care if you turned out to be a loser and have a shitty life?" I asked.

"Because . . . they love me," Harry replied, as if realizing this for the first time in a long while.

And that's all it took. The rest of the session continued in a cooperative and collaborative fashion, free of vicious attacks and underhanded shots and unvoiced rage. The Franklins actually talked with each other like people who cared about each other, instead of tearing at each other like rabid dogs.

After that breakthrough I started using this technique to bridge communication gaps and repair rifts among law partners, senior managers, managers, and subordinates. (You'll see a good example at the start of Chapter 5, where I employed it with two warring attorneys.) I call this approach "empathogenic communication" because it instantly fosters empathy among people who've previously only known antipathy or even outright hatred. Think of it as the Empathy Jolt.

■ How It Works

Empathy is a sensory experience; that is, it activates the sensory part of your nervous system, including the mirror neurons we've talked about. Anger, on the other hand, is a motor action—usually a reaction to some perceived hurt or injury by another person. So by taking people out of anger and shifting them into an empathic behavior, the Empathy Jolt moves them from the motor brain to the sensory brain.

To put it another way, anger and empathy—like matter and antimatter—can't exist in the same place at the same time. Let one in, and you have to let the other one go. So when you shift a blamer into empathy, you stop the person's angry ranting dead in its tracks.

And what about the person who's on the defensive? Initially, this human punching bag is frustrated because no matter what he or she is trying to mirror outward——*I'm sorry, I'm confused, I'm scared, I had a good reason for what I did*—the ignorant blamer is blind to it. As a result, the person who's under attack is usually in a state of quiet, barely controlled rage.

Suddenly and unexpectedly, however, the blamer knows just how sad, angry, scared, or lonely the defender feels and spontaneously turns into an ally. When the defender feels understood by the blamer and that they are on the same side, there's nothing to defend against. The defender's wall, and with it his unspoken rage and frustration, dissipates. The relief from no longer feeling "fear or loathing" toward the blamer spontaneously triggers a tremendous rush of gratitude and—miraculously—the person's quiet rage turns into forgiveness and, beyond that, a willingness to work toward solutions.

■ WHEN TO EMPLOY THE EMPATHY JOLT

The Empathy Jolt is a powerful intervention to use when two people in your life are beating on each other brutally instead of communicating—or when at least one person is more interested in attacking than in listening. Use it at the first sign that a conflict is getting out of control.

Here's an example:

MANAGER OF A SOFTWARE TEAM: We've targeted this release for next week, but I hear there's a problem.

SIMON: Yeah, there's a problem. Kim didn't give me enough time to work on it. Her targets aren't realistic. Nobody could get this done in time.

KIM (FURIOUS): Simon could if he did what I ask of him. We're late because he spent three extra days adding a bunch of graphics bells and whistles that nobody cares about. We have to sell this product but instead we have a bunch of worthless features and no product to sell. Don't blame me for this mess.

SOFTWARE MANAGER: Okay. Before we talk about what's going on with the release, I'd like to do something first. I know that both of you are extraordinarily good at what you do. In fact, you're two of the strongest performers I've ever worked with. And I also know that it's very hard for you to work together. So I'd like to ask each of you a question, with the goal of seeing if we can make this situation work better for both of you.

KIM AND SIMON (BOTH DEFENSIVELY): Okay.

SOFTWARE MANAGER: Let's start with you, Kim. Here's the question: If I were to ask Simon what frustrates him most about working with you, what would he say?

KIM (SURPRISED BY THE QUESTION): Um. Well. Uh . . . I think he might say that I don't respect his talent. Or that I'm more interested in setting deadlines than in making the product as good as it could be.

SOFTWARE MANAGER: So, what does that make him want to do?

KIM: Get mad. Because—look, I know he's really interested in making this product the best one on the market and he can't. And I understand that, I really do, but the company doesn't work that way.

SOFTWARE MANAGER: Thanks. I appreciate that. And now I'd like to ask the same question of Simon. Simon, If I were to ask Kim what frustrates her most about working with you, what would she say?

SIMON (DISARMED BY KIM'S UNDERSTANDING): Well . . . um . . . okay, I think she'd say that upper management expects her to meet deadlines and she gets blamed if we're late because I spend time adding stuff that management didn't ask for. And I really do understand that. I mean, to me it's wrong to send out a product that's not as good as it could be, but I can see how that's a problem for Kim.

SOFTWARE MANAGER: And how does that make her feel?

SIMON: Probably scared that they'll can her. Or mad at me for screwing things up for her.

SOFTWARE MANAGER: Thanks for answering that so honestly. Now, I know that for right now we want to focus on getting this release done as quickly as we can. So let's work out a schedule and see if we can still meet the target date. But would you two be willing to meet afterward and see if there's a way to get Simon's goal of making the best possible product to mesh better with Kim's need to meet our targets? Because I'm confident that you can come up with some good solutions together.

When you use the Empathy Jolt, avoid the mistake of interjecting your own opinions during the process—even if they're positive ones ("I certainly agree about what you're saying about Simon's talents"). Your goal is to get two people to mirror each other, and they can't do that if you're standing between them. So facilitate, but don't butt in.

Also, understand that you're not trying to solve the problem that's on the table right now (a kid who's violating curfew, a coworker who's missing deadlines, etc.). Instead, you're shifting people to a place where *they* can solve the problem—and the next one that comes up, and the one after that.

Do this right and you'll all have fewer problems to solve, because people who experience an Empathy Jolt will have less desire in the future to rip each other apart and more desire to make things go right for each other. That's because they've actually "been" each other, for at least a moment, and now they know what it feels like.

■ THE POWER OF ANALOGY

Often you can use the Empathy Jolt to get another person to understand your own feelings. For example, say to a coworker who frequently leaves you in the lurch on projects, "Isn't it frustrating when a client promises to send a check on time and then doesn't, and we need to worry about whether the person's going to stiff us—but we still need to be polite because we can't risk offending the person?"

When the person says something like "Very," say, "And doesn't that make you feel angry and even scared about doing business with the person?"

After the person says "Yes," gently say, "Knowing how it feels to be blown off that way, would you want to do that to someone else?"

Most likely you'll get a "No, of course not," which is when you can say, "Well, you know, that's how I feel when I need to count on you to get a project done and I'm not sure you'll come through. I don't want to hurt your feelings because I respect and like you, but I feel frustrated and scared when I'm not sure I can count on you."

Odds are, the person will take this lesson to heart—and your brief Empathy Jolt will earn you far more cooperation in the future.

■ USING THE EMPATHY JOLT ON YOURSELF ■

Are you an ignorant blamer? The truth is that we all are, at one point or another in our lives. If you frequently find yourself in vicious arguments where you wield anger and blame as weapons, take action: Awaken your own empathy.

Here's how.

1. Think of someone who frequently frustrates, angers, hurts, or disappoints you. This may be someone in your family, someone at work, or a friend.

2. Imagine that person doing one of the things that frustrates you. Select a behavior that, on an aggravation scale of 1 to 10, is at least an 8. Get this picture fully in your mind and be conscious of how it makes you feel as you think about it.

3. Now, put yourself in the other person's shoes. Imagine what the person would say if I asked what angers, hurts, or frustrates him or her most about *you*. Imagine you are the other person and say what this person would probably answer, such as, you're hypercritical, you're judgmental, you always want to play the martyr, or you're controlling. Be honest about the negative things you do in this relationship.

4. Next, imagine that I ask this person how much it upsets him or her to be so frustrated and upset with you. Again, put yourself in this person's shoes and say, "A lot."

5. Now imagine me asking the other person, "Can you describe something hurtful that this person (you) has done?" Think about any hurtful acts you've committed in this relationship, and how they made the other person feel, and answer as if you're that person.

6. Finally, on that same scale of 1 to 10, rate how you now score your level of aggravation with this person.

What happened? Most likely, you felt angry at the beginning of this exercise, but the intensity of your anger dropped as you put yourself in the other person's shoes. Typically, when I do this exercise with audiences, they start out at 8 or 9 and end up at 3 or 4. That's because you can't experience what another person is feeling *and* be angry at the person at the same moment in time.

So the next time you feel like ripping into someone who's making you angry, take a deep breath, find a quiet place, and do this exercise first. Odds are you'll save yourself, and the other person, a lot of grief.

➡ *Usable Insight*
You can't be curious and on the attack at the same moment.

➡ *Action Step*
To make empathy come more naturally to you, give yourself an Empathy Jolt every day or so. For instance, when a coworker you don't like much is on the phone with a difficult client, observe the situation and ask yourself, "How would I feel if I were him right now? Would this conversation make me angry, frustrated, or unhappy?" Or if your boss is brusquer than usual one day, ask yourself: "How would I feel if I had all of her responsibilities and worries today?" The more you do this, the less stress and frustration you'll feel with the people around you—and the better you'll be at getting through to them.

15

THE REVERSE PLAY, EMPATHY JOLT #2

*Benefit: Move a resistant underachiever
all the way to the "willing to do"
stage by creating empathy.*

Humility is the surest sign of strength.
—THOMAS MERTON, AUTHOR AND TRAPPIST MONK

Vince is a slacker. He has more than enough smarts to do his job as a legal assistant, but he cuts corners. Frequently he does sloppy work or shoves projects off on other people. While his coworkers stay late to meet deadlines, he leaves early.

The firm that hired Vince thought they were snagging a real asset, but Vince is turning out to be a problem instead. And management is disappointed.

One day, Vince's boss calls him into the office. Vince worries: Did the higher-ups finally notice that he wasn't pulling his weight? He's feeling a mix of defensiveness, fear, and anger.

Tyrell, Vince's boss, meets him at the office door, asks him to take a seat and offers him a cup of coffee. And then he surprises the hell out of Vince.

Tyrell says exactly what I've told him to say: "I'm sorry. I think there must be things I do that frustrate you a great deal, and I'd like to apologize for them. Here's what I think those things are. . . ."

> A half-hour later, Vince is back at his desk. He's working harder than he has since the day he got hired. And he's happy about it.

What did Tyrell do to transform Vince from a problem to a power-house in 30 minutes? He used an approach that takes everyone by surprise. I call it the Reverse Play (because it's exactly the opposite of what people expect), and it's an in-your-face version of the Empathy Jolt I described in Chapter 14.

I strongly recommend the Reverse Play if you're dealing with someone who has the skills and ability to do a job, but isn't giving 100 percent. Here's how you do it.

1. First, tell the person that you'd like to get together for 10 minutes. Set a time when you can have the person's undivided attention; if the person wants to meet with you immediately, respectfully say, "No, you're in the middle of something and it isn't a life-or-death matter. It'll wait until you're not distracted by anything else."

2. Prepare yourself for the meeting by thinking of three specific, legitimate ways in which the other person may be disappointed or frustrated with you. For instance: *Tina thinks I always give her the least interesting projects. She's probably frustrated because I didn't give her a big enough budget to get the equipment she'd like. And she's probably mad because she inherited lots of problems created by the last person in her job, and sometimes I blame her for them.* It doesn't matter how frustrated or disappointed *you* are; set all of your own issues to one side, and think like the other person.

3. When the time for your meeting arrives, the other person will be expecting you to criticize or be confrontational. Instead, say, "You're probably waiting for me to lay out a list of complaints, like I usually do. However, I was thinking about the reasons why *you* might be disappointed in *me*. You're probably afraid to tell me about these things, because you figure I'll get defensive. I think these things are. . . ." Then lay out the three things that you suspect disappoint the person most about you.

4. End with, "Is that true? If not, what *are* the things that most frustrate you about me?" Then listen to whatever the person says, pause, and say, "And how much do those things bother you?"

5. After the person replies (probably rather timidly), respond sincerely with, "Really . . . I didn't know and I guess I didn't want to know. I'm sorry and I'll try to do better in the future."

6. Then stop. If the person asks, "Is there anything else?," say sincerely, "No, that's all I wanted to say—I really appreciate what you've told me." If the person persists and asks why you've initiated this conversation, respond with something like this: "I know I make mistakes, and I know that people may be hesitant to point them out to me. And I know I can do a better job myself, and create a better work environment, if I'm aware of what I'm doing wrong."

Why should you do this, when it's the last thing you want to do? Because it works when other approaches don't. Ignore a slacker, and the problem will continue and probably escalate. Confront the person, expecting to receive an apology and a promise to reform, and you're likely to create an enemy who'll look for every opportunity to covertly work against you.

But do the unexpected by apologizing yourself, and something very different occurs: You shift a person instantly out of defensive mode and cause the individual to mirror your humility and concern. Taking responsibility for your actions and committing to correct your faults in the future also demonstrates tremendous graciousness, generosity, and poise, and turns you into a person worthy of respect.

As a result, that same person who's always circumvented or ignored or sniped at you will dramatically shift course. You've caused this person to respect and admire you and, as a result, the person will now worry about disappointing you. Often, you'll see an instant change in attitude and work performance as a result.

You can use this same technique at home with children (with whom it's particularly effective), as well as with friends and family. For example, watch how Dana uses it to salvage a friendship with a once-close friend who's disappointed her more than once.

SHARON (ARRIVING LATE FOR LUNCH AND ALREADY DEFENSIVE): Hi, sorry I'm late. Just add it to the list of things you're probably mad about. I know you're pissed off that I missed your party for Joe, and I forgot to return that dress you wanted to wear. . . .

DANA: No, don't worry, this isn't a bitchfest. Actually, I wanted to do just the opposite. I've been thinking about our friendship, and I've realized that I haven't been as good a friend as I should be lately.

SHARON: What?

DANA: Yeah, I'm betting that you're getting tired of me always complaining about little stuff like the dress. And not appreciating that you're more spontaneous than me, and you don't always like me to plan your life. And talking too much about Joe and me, and not paying enough attention to you. . . .

SHARON: Whoa, girl, it's okay! Well, yeah, maybe some of that stuff bugs me, but I don't expect you to be perfect. But hey, since you mention it, I do appreciate you understanding how I feel. And I guess I do feel a little hurt when you bring Joe along every time we get together, when sometimes I'd like to just have a girl talk.

DANA: I'm sorry. Does that drive you crazy?

SHARON (LAUGHING): Yeah, but probably not as crazy as me canceling on you all the time. I'm really sorry about that—I'm trying to get more organized, but you know me and my ADHD. I'll really try to do better. . . . our friendship means a lot to me, and I need to work harder at it.

In addition to using a Reverse Play to disarm and remotivate a recalcitrant subordinate or friend, you can use it to repair a relationship that *you* have messed up.

I did just that with a former best friend from my medical internship. Young and oversensitive, I'd felt hurt by something innocent this person had done. As a result, I'd failed to stay in touch with him when, after our internship, he moved 90 miles away.

In a nutshell, we lost contact for nearly 20 years. Then one day I realized that I was wrong for holding onto this grudge for so long, and I was violating my commitment to not be a grudge holder after seeing so many unforgiving people grow up to be unhappy and even bitter.

I called my friend out of the blue and said, "Frank, I'm calling because I think I've been holding onto a minor grudge against you for all these years for something I can't even remember. I don't think it was anything you did, but my oversensitive reaction caused me to lose contact with you. So I decided to call you and see how you and your family are, because we were the best of friends during our internship."

Now, Frank was one of the most normal, upbeat, liked, and respected people during our internship (he won the best intern award), and he hadn't changed. So he responded as if we'd never stopped being friends, "Hey Mark, great to hear from you. I never thought there was any rift between us, I just thought we moved away and got busy with our lives."

After briefly catching up, we finished the call a few minutes later. Talk about feeling foolish—I felt like an incredibly neurotic psychiatrist (you're thinking, "Aren't they all?").

But that's not the end of the story. My call and my apology must have touched Frank, because two days later he called and said, "Hey, Mark, what are you doing this weekend? If you're around, I'd like to bring my family down to Los Angeles and come and meet yours."

While I used the Reverse Play to counter a grudge I'd created myself, typically you'll use it on another person who's creating a problem. The Reverse Play can move a person from defiance to cooperation in a heartbeat, but make sure you choose the right targets when you employ this approach. The approach works best with people who are "trainable"—those who just need a little incentive to shape up. It works less well (or not at all) with the takers and narcissists I talk about in Chapter 11, because they're not into reciprocating.

However, if you're not sure whether to continue a relationship or abandon it, you can try using the Reverse Play as a diagnostic test. People who respond to it by boosting their performance and working to earn your respect are keepers. As for those who continue to disappoint you instead of reciprocating your humility, don't go ballistic and strike back as you'll be tempted to do. Instead, just say "goodbye."

➡ *Usable Insight*
An ounce of apology is worth a pound of resentment and a ton of "acting out by underperforming."

➡ *Action Step*
Think of someone who's disappointing you and invite the person to lunch or dinner. Before you go, rate your disappointment with the person on a 1-to-5 scale (with 5 being "extremely disappoint-ed"). During your meeting, use the Reverse Play to apologize for anything you've done that might have annoyed, upset, or offended the other person.

One month after your lunch, think about the person's behavior since your meeting and rate your level of disappointment with the person. Is it significantly lower? Then your approach worked. Is it the same or higher? If so, think about easing that person out of your life—because you're probably dealing with a narcissist who'll cause you nothing but problems in the future.

16

"DO YOU *REALLY* BELIEVE THAT?"

*Benefit: Move a person who's "over the top"
from resistance to listening by
lowering the person's anger or fear.*

An exaggeration is a truth
that has lost its temper.
—KAHLIL GIBRAN, POET AND PHILOSOPHER

H ere's a fun little trick I owe to my friend Scott Regberg, whose Los Angeles firm, Regberg & Associates, produces high-profile events ranging from televised presidential debates to major national conferences. If you've ever participated in that kind of planning, you know it takes nerves of steel and the organizational ability of General Patton.

But above all, as Scott can tell you, pulling off huge events without a hitch (and making it look effortless) requires the ability to communicate effectively and keep people calm when deadlines are looming. That includes clients, planners, designers, graphic artists, and hundreds of other people from the top to the bottom.

One thing Scott is particularly good at when it comes to keeping everyone on track is soothing the types of people who go into a tailspin over minor, readily handled problems. (If you've ever planned a wedding reception or bar mitzvah, you know the kind of people I'm talking about.) Here's what Scott does. When a person launches into an out-of-control rant about how awful the problem is and how it's the end of the world, etc., etc., Scott simply says, calmly: "Do you *really* believe that?"

This is a highly effective question because when you ask it in a calm way, it causes most people who use hyperbole or exaggeration to recant and restate their position. Typically, they backpedal by saying something like, "Well, not really, but I *am* very frustrated about things." Then you can respond, "I understand that, but I need to know what the truth is, because if what you say is totally true then we have a serious problem and need to address it." By this time, they're in retreat and the power has shifted to you.

The trick to this approach is to ask the question ("Do you *really* believe that?") not in a hostile or degrading manner, but very calmly and in a straightforward way. Your intent is not to antagonize the other person, but rather to make the person stop and realize, "I really am making a mountain out of a molehill. I must sound like a jackass."

Often, all you need is that one sentence—"Do you *really* believe that?"—plus a follow-up question or two. For example:

YOUR PARTNER: God, I can't believe we're arguing about money again. Screw it. I can't win because every time I tell you I'm worried about money, you go out and buy something and tell me I'm just being cheap. You won't be happy until we're bankrupt!

YOU: Do you really believe that? That *every time* you tell me you're worried about money, I go out and buy something and tell you you're cheap—and that I won't be happy until we're bankrupt?

YOUR PARTNER: Yeah. 'Cuz that's how you act. Well, okay, you don't exactly do that. But that's what it seems like.

YOU: I understand what you're saying, but I really need to know if you think I don't care about our money situation and *really* want to bankrupt us. Because if that's the case, I think we have some serious misunderstandings to clear up.

YOUR PARTNER (NOW LESS HOSTILE): Jeez, that's not what I meant. Okay, I was exaggerating. It's just that I feel so frustrated with you whenever I try to have a conversation with you about one of my worries and you blow me off.

You: Whenever as in always.

Your partner (smiling, caught in hyperbole again): Okay, not always, just a lot. And it does frustrate me.

At this point, the "tit for tat" argument where you're talking *at* and *over* each other is quickly becoming a "give and take" conversation where you're beginning to talk *with* each other.

If the person you're dealing with is a chronic whiner and you're in a position of authority in which you don't need to worry about jeopardizing your job or a relationship, you can try the "steroids" version of this technique. Here's an example:

Bill, a high-powered car salesman, bursting into his manager's office unannounced: What do I gotta do to get a frickin' purchase order okayed around here? All the frickin' people here don't know what the f#%& they're doing! They're all imbeciles and they're all incompetent!

Frank (his sales manager): Do you *really* believe that?

Bill (caught off guard and not even recalling what he said in the heat of anger): Believe what?

Frank (in a measured, firm, calm tone): Do you really believe that absolutely everyone who works here doesn't know what they're doing and that they are *all*—each and every one—imbeciles and incompetent? Are you saying that there is not one single person who works here who knows what they are doing?

Bill (caught with his exaggeration up and his pants down): Well not absolutely everyone, but it really is difficult to get things when you need them.

Frank (continuing his inquiry): No I mean it, Bill. If every single person who works here is incompetent, we have some very big problems, and I'm going to need your help in rooting them out and solving them.

Bill (calming down slightly): No, c'mon, you know, I was just really pissed off. Not everyone is incompetent.

Frank: I understand you were pissed off, but I really need your help to solve this problem. When do you think we could do that?

BILL: No, really. I'm too busy. I was frustrated and getting things off my chest.

FRANK: Oh, well I'm glad you're feeling better. So tell me exactly what you need us to fix, because I really don't want you to have to get so frustrated.

BILL (BEGINNING TO CALMLY MAKE SOME REQUESTS FOR HELP): First of all, I need this. . . .

Notice how quickly Bill backs down. What's more, he's likely to remember this encounter the next time he thinks about going ballistic—and that memory will be a strong reminder to keep his temper under control.

Of course, every few years you may be shocked when someone responds to your question "Do you *really* believe that?" with a very firm "yes." If so, be reachable yourself and listen to what the person has to say. A person who's brave enough to say "yes" to this question, and to stick by that answer, probably has some legitimate issues and will be happier and more productive if you iron those issues out. So no matter which answer you get—"yes" or "no"—you'll solve some big problems with this simple question.

➡ *Usable Insight*
Before you worry about solving someone else's problem, find out if there really *is* a problem.

➡ *Action Step*
Think of someone you deal with who often uses hyperbole to make a point, exhausts you with his or her histrionics, and makes you want to run in the other direction each time the two of you meet.

The next time this person starts in on an overheated rant, simply let it slide off your back. Then pause for a count of five and say, "Do you really believe that?" Watch the person backpedal, and then pin the person down about the details of the actual problem (if one really exists).

17

THE POWER OF "HMMM. . . ."

Benefit: Calm a person who's upset or angry, moving the person from resisting to listening and then from listening to considering.

Your most unhappy customers
are your greatest source of learning.
—BILL GATES, MICROSOFT CHAIRMAN

L et's say you're in sales. Your company, worried about slumping revenues, wants me to train you and your colleagues to use my techniques to increase your sales. You're not happy about that—and you're too pissed off right now to feel like beating around the bush about it.

Over lunch, you say to me, "I don't know why I need to learn all this crap about getting through to people. Why can't I just do the job I'm trained to do? Why can't I just ask customers what they're looking for and how much they want to spend, and then show them where to pay? I just don't have the time or energy to learn all this shrink stuff."

You fully expect me to get mad or defensive. Because after all, it's my "shrink stuff" you're talking about.

But I don't. Instead, I say, "Hmmm," in a *tell-me-more* tone of voice.

So you continue, "I really hate having to learn this stuff to get sales. This has nothing to do with what I'm competent at.

Besides, I already read some books on this stuff. They made sense, and I tried a couple of things and they actually worked. But after awhile I forgot to do them, so it didn't last."

"Really," I say. And you're surprised, because it sounds like I still want you to say more. So you do.

"Yeah," you say. "It's frustrating. I mean, maybe this stuff comes naturally to you, but I'm a salesperson. And with all the pressure and the workload and everything else I'm juggling, it's hard to remember some idea I read in a book six months ago."

"And so . . . ," I reply understandingly, invitingly, but leaving the responsibility of where this conversation is going up to you.

You continue, "And so . . . well, okay, I know I'm starting to sound like a whiner. And I know that this stuff worked when I tried it before. Maybe what it boils down to is that I need to make a decision. I guess if I try your ideas and find out they really work, then I need to decide if this is the time when I persevere and keep using them. Then I won't have to keep learning this stuff all over again."

I respond, "You've spent a lot of time trying to use this stuff in a hit-or-miss way and you've gotten hit-or-miss results. I can understand why you're frustrated, because that has to be a drag."

"Yeah it is," you reply, "but look, I know I've done it to myself. I hate it when I sound like a victim. I should just put my mind to it and do it and commit to doing it every day until it sticks."

"You know," I offer, "Here's one thing that might help. A tip I give my clients is that if you keep doing the same behavior for 21 days it turns into a habit that's easier to maintain. It's kind of like dental flossing." You think about that for a second, and give me a nod.

"So what do you want to do?" I ask. You pause, thinking about your situation: slumping sales, argumentative customers, the bills you can't pay if you don't meet your quotas. You fiddle for a minute with your salad. And then you conclude, "It's not what I want to do—it's what I *need* to do."

I let that hang in the air while I drink my coffee. Then I ask, "How will you know when it's finally time for you to do it?"

> You think it over. And you say, "It's probably now or never."
>
> "Okay," I say. And before the main course arrives, we're two allies agreeing to work together.

What just happened?

You started out mad, frustrated, and defensive, and you expected things to go downhill from there. After each angry thing you said, you paused, instinctively waiting for me to lecture you, confront you, or focus on your counterproductive behavior. If I'd done any of those things, you probably would have dug your heels in and argued with me—even if you secretly agreed with what I said.

So I did just the opposite. Instead of shutting you down, I encouraged you to go deeper by using words like "Hmmm," "Really," and "And so." Each time I did that, you calmed down a little more. As a result, by the end of our talk, you weren't trying to tell me why you'd fail. In fact, you were working hard to convince me that you'd succeed.

"Hmmm . . ." is a tool to use when you're facing a person who's angry, defensive, and sure you're the bad guy. It works in a wide range of settings—everything from a hostage crisis to an angry customer scenario—because it rapidly turns a potential brawl into a cooperative dialogue. Here's why.

Most people do exactly the wrong thing when confronted by an angry or upset person. They say well-intentioned things, such as "okay, just calm down"—or they lose it and get angry themselves. ("Oh yeah? Well, you may think my ideas are just crap, but you're wrong, and I can prove it.") Both of these approaches generally have disastrous results. Make the other person angry, and you'll get into a shouting match. Ask the person politely to calm down, and you'll send the condescending and infuriating message: "I'm sane, and you're a flaming nutball." The response, in either case, will be a dramatic shift to resistance on the other person's part.

"Hmmm . . . ," conversely, is a potent deescalator. When you use this approach, you're not trying to shut someone up; instead, you're telling the other person, "You're important to me and so is your problem." And that brings us right back to those mirror neurons.

When people go on the attack it's usually because they feel (rightly or wrongly) that they've been treated poorly. That's especially true if you're dealing with angry and frustrated customers. Often such people feel hurt in many areas of life but save their "road rage" for outbursts that they believe won't get them fired, divorced, or arrested—like kicking the dog or yelling at you.

Becoming defensive or counterattacking simply reinforces the idea that you think these people are wrong and unimportant (and stupid), which amplifies their mirror neuron gap and fuels their fire. When you make a counterintuitive move and encourage them to talk, you do the opposite: You mirror respect and interest, and they feel compelled to send the same message back.

"Hmmm . . ." is what I call a "relationship deepener." It tells people that what they say is important, worth listening to, and worthy of some sort of action. You'll notice, however, that it *commits you to nothing.* The sole purpose is to calm a person to the point where you can identify the actual problem and come up with a realistic solution.

For these reasons I recommend "hmmm . . ." as your first line of defense if you're dealing with a client or customer meltdown. Here's an example of how it works.

> CUSTOMER (BELLIGERENTLY): Your company has sold me a piece of junk for the last time! Your products stink, your service is worse, and you're just a bunch of greedy liars.
>
> YOU (IN AN ENCOURAGING VOICE, AS IF YOU WANT TO HEAR MORE): Hmmm. . . .
>
> CUSTOMER (ANGRILY): What do you mean, "Hmmm!?"
>
> YOU (FIRMLY AND CALMLY): I was just thinking how important it is that we fix, correct, or do something about this as soon as possible or else it's just going to get worse. And I don't think worse would be a good place to go. Don't you agree?
>
> CUSTOMER (BEGINNING TO BACKTRACK AND CALM DOWN): Er, uh, well, yeah. But I'll be amazed if you actually help me. You have no idea how much trouble I've had with you.
>
> YOU (INVITINGLY): Tell me more.

CUSTOMER: Really? You got all day? Well, okay, you asked for it. For one thing, the last GPS unit you sent me didn't work. And when I sent it back for repairs, you gave me back an old rebuilt unit that was all scratched up and looked like crap.

YOU: I can see why you were upset. What else can you tell me about the problems you've had with us?

CUSTOMER (MELLOWING): Well . . . um . . . most of the other stuff was actually pretty minor. And they did exchange that crappy unit for a better one when I complained. But now this unit I ordered for my wife's car isn't working. And when I tried sending an e-mail about the problem, they never replied.

YOU: Alright, let's make sure we get that problem handled as quickly as we can. I think it probably has to do with a software glitch we've corrected, and we can fix it with a patch you can download. In case that doesn't work, I'm going to give you my direct line so we can find another solution. But before we get to that, is there anything else you'd like to share about your experiences with us?

CUSTOMER: Um. Just that I'm not too impressed with your company's customer service. Well, except for now. Maybe it's getting better. And hey, I'm sorry that I yelled at you because I know that what happened before isn't your fault.

YOU: No problem at all. I can understand what you're going through. Now, let's figure out what's going on with your new unit. . . .

Read through that dialogue again, and you'll spot an interesting detail. Initially your customer's bullets are aimed straight at your heart: Your products stink; your service stinks; you're a liar; you suck. But after a few minutes, things subtly start to change. Somewhere along the line, your customer becomes mad at "them" or "your company." Why? Because the customer now feels like you two are on the same side and doesn't want to hurt you. Once that shift occurs, you can stop ducking for cover and start working together to solve the problem.

Because "hmmm . . ." can turn a person from enemy to ally so quickly, you're also likely to find it extraordinarily effective in your personal life—especially in those tinderbox encounters where one wrong word can spark a conflagration. One caution, however: You're more likely to react viscerally to a partner's or child's rage than you are to the anger of someone you don't know, so get your head in the right place before you open your mouth. Once you've done the "Oh F#@& to OK" Speed Drill I describe in Chapter 3, and you're sure you have yourself under control, try something like this.

> YOUR PARTNER: I can't believe it. I mean, I just can't believe it. You promised we'd finally get away for a weekend and now you're backing out. That's so like you.
>
> YOU: Hmmm. . . .
>
> YOUR PARTNER: Hmmm? What's that supposed to mean?
>
> YOU: Just that I know how important this trip was to you, and I'm really sorry the project ran overtime and I can't get away.
>
> YOUR PARTNER: You always say something like that. It's always some life-or-death thing at work. I hate it.
>
> YOU: And so. . . .
>
> YOUR PARTNER: And so I wish you'd get a different job where there's not so much pressure. Or I wish you'd stop making plans when you know you'll have to break them. Or . . . I don't know. I wish crap like this didn't always happen. And I know you do too, and I know you're stuck with this job right now. And I guess it's no fun for you either. I'm sorry, but I'm just really angry right now. Sorry I went off on you.

Once again, you'll notice that your goal isn't to solve the specific problem you're facing (although it can sometimes happen). Instead, it's to avoid talking *at* each other, move beyond talking *to* each other, and with luck end up talking *with* each other. When that happens, you reach a place where you and the other person can work together as allies to handle an issue instead of devolving into hurtful attacks on each other.

"Hmmm" is just one of many phrases that can rapidly defuse a conversation that's escalating. Others include: "Really?" "And so . . . ," " "Tell me more," "Then what happened?" and "What else can you tell me?" Of all these, "Hmmm . . ." is my favorite opening line because it catches people off guard—and catching people off guard is a good way to stop a meltdown. Move a person from hostility to mild confusion and already you've moved one step in the right direction.

However, it doesn't matter which exact words or phrases you pick. The key is how you use them: not to argue, defend, or make excuses, but to say: "You're important. Your problem is important. And I'm listening." Get that message across, and your problem—no matter what it is—is already more than halfway to a solution.

➡ *Usable Insight*
Don't get *defensive;* go *deeper.*

➡ *Action Step*
Still not sure about the "Hmmm . . ." technique? Okay. Then this time, I'll do something different and take the action step myself, by imagining still another conversation with you. Here's how it might go.

You: This sounds like a bunch of psychological crap. Why can't you give me something I can use!?

Me: Hmmm. . . .

You: Don't try your "Hmmm" b.s. on me!

Me: You sound angry—or is it just frustrated?

You: It's more frustrated. I have to get through to some people, and I've been hitting my head against a wall and the pressure's getting to me.

Me: Really. . . .

You: Yeah, if I don't get through to these potential customers, I won't get the sale I need to meet my numbers.

Me: Tell me more.

You: "With this crazy economy, everyone at my company is under pressure to bring in more sales and if we don't we're just asking to get laid off."

Me: So you're scared that might happen to you.

YOU: Yeah, I'm getting more and more uptight—which is making me impatient with everyone and everything, including reading this book."

ME: How scared are you?

YOU (A LITTLE CHOKED UP): Real scared.

ME (PAUSING TO LET YOU EXHALE): So even though you've been scared before and bounced back, you're worried that if you're fired you won't bounce back this time.

YOU: Kinda, but I *have* always bounced back. In fact I'm thinking if I do well, I'll keep this job; but if I don't do well, I'll find another job just like I always have—and maybe in a company that's not going through the same tough times. I mean, I am a great salesperson.

ME: So it's not you, it's your company. It's tough to sell stuff that customers don't need or want, but when you're selling something that people want, you do okay.

YOU: I do better than okay; I do great!

ME: And so?

YOU: And so I have nothing to lose. If I do the best I can, and it doesn't work out, it's not me—it's my company, and I *can* go elsewhere.

ME: Hmmm.

YOU (LAUGHING): "There you go with that 'hmmm' again.

ME: Maybe it worked with you.

YOU (RELAXED): And maybe *I* need to read this chapter over again.

18

THE STIPULATION GAMBIT

*Benefit: Move a person from considering to
"willing to do" by neutralizing your weak points.*

Conceal a flaw, and the world
will imagine the worst.
—MARCUS VALERIUS MARTIAL, ROMAN POET

If you're familiar with courtroom procedures, you know that lawyers do something they call "stipulation." It means they agree up-front on something.

For instance, if a lawyer stipulates that John Doe's fingerprints were on the gun that killed his mother-in-law, then everyone agrees to that fact. The other lawyer doesn't need to call in experts to testify to this, and Doe's lawyer can move on to the next step: proving that the shooting was justified.

Why is stipulation a smart technique? Because when people already know (or will quickly find out) the problem that you're admitting to, your best move is to get it out of the way. Even better, you can often transform that problem into a powerful asset.

Frequently we invest a great deal of energy in hiding weaknesses even when they're clear to anyone who meets us. The result: We make people uncomfortable, because they're forced to actively ignore the problem and focus a great deal of attention on avoiding talking about it. When we make them uncomfortable, their mirror neurons can't create an emotional connection, because they're actively avoiding that connection. Their own minds aren't saying, "Reach out to this person." They're saying: "Be careful. Don't trust this guy. If he's hiding this, he's probably hiding something else."

The solution? If there's a big, glaring problem standing between you and reaching another person, stipulate to it.

Here's an example. I recently received a note from a young man who reads my column in the *Los Angeles Times*. He said, "I am twenty-six and I have a s-t-u-t-t-e-r-i-n-g problem. The worst part of it is never knowing when it will rear its ugly head. Not knowing adds pressure, which of course brings it on."

He was good at what he did, but he didn't get jobs—and he knew it was because his stuttering (and people's well-intentioned efforts to pretend not to notice it) made interviewers highly uncomfortable. Despite the Americans with Disabilities Act, job interviewers can always find ways to disqualify a candidate, and that's exactly what kept happening to this young man.

I advised him to try an approach that worked well for a patient of mine named Joe. Joe was in the same boat: He went to interview after interview, but never got hired because of his stuttering.

I told Joe not to stress out by trying to avoid stuttering—something that never worked. Instead, I told him to say this at the start of each interview: "I have a stuttering problem. The worst part of it is that I never know when it will happen. When it does people are caught off guard, feel badly for me, don't know what to do, and become distracted. If it happens while we're talking, the best thing to do is to bear with me and if you and I are lucky it will come and go. If it doesn't, we'll just have to do the best we can. I apologize in advance for whatever inconvenience this causes you."

By talking about his stuttering up front, Joe eliminated the element of surprise and felt calmer and more in control. Better yet, he earned the appreciation and respect of other people for the poise he showed, his anticipation of their discomfort, and his helpful advice for handling that discomfort.

Years later, after his stuttering had nearly gone away, Joe told me, "I still tell people I used to stutter a lot and tell them what to do if it happens now, because it's one of the most effective ways to quickly gain people's respect *and* to start them rooting for me."

Stipulation helps you neutralize other types of problems as well. As a psychiatrist in the business field I often fight an uphill battle as soon as business audiences find out what my profession is. When they hear what I do for a living, I can see the eye rolls and feel the skepticism from many of them.

To counter this, I use my own version of Joe's speech. I start out by saying: "I am a psychiatrist without an MBA or formal business training. I know that my profession has many doubters and detractors. But here are some things I've learned to do in my career. I've assisted grown children in deciding to put their terminally ill parents on morphine, I've gotten couples who hadn't slept in the same bedroom for years to have sex again, I've convinced partners who are nearly coming to blows to listen to each other, I've helped lawyers who have completely burned bridges with clients to unburn them, and I've prevented the founding partner of a blown-up hedge fund from foolishly and tragically ending his life . . . so I do know something about getting through to people. And I would imagine that getting through to people is something you need to do every day."

That's a lot to say just to get people to listen to me, but it works. In two minutes, I take a crowd that's hostile or at best skeptical and turn it into a rapt group of people who are thinking, "Hey—this guy probably has something really important to say."

This same approach will work for you, but only if you do it right. Here are the three keys: *Get in* (quickly and efficiently describe the issue), *neutralize the problem* (by explaining how to handle it or why it isn't really a problem), and *get out* (move on to the next topic —do not linger or go into excess detail). Here's an example.

JOB INTERVIEWER: So, tell me about your education and experience.

SOFTWARE DEVELOPER: Well, I'm guessing that I will be the only person you consider for this job who doesn't have a degree in the field. That's because I was more-or-less "born into it"—I wrote my first software program when I was just nine, and my parents were both programmers so I think I was born a geek. I actually got my first job at sixteen, because one of our neighbors found out I could design databases, and he hired me on the spot. He's retired, but I've listed him as a reference and his store is still using my code today.

JOB INTERVIEWER: Wow.

YOU: I also have a list of other clients who'll be glad to talk with you about my work. . . .

When you stipulate to a potential problem or flaw, do it in a confident and unselfconscious way. The more relaxed you are, the more relaxed the person you're communicating with will be—and the easier it will be for both of you to focus on your message.

Stipulation takes courage, but the payoff is big. When you use this approach, you'll turn defects into assets and empower people to view you as a person rather than as a problem. What's more, you may find to your great surprise that the problem that's been holding you back is a key to moving you forward.

■ THE COMEBACK KID ■

Several years ago, I gave an inspirational talk to a group of lawyers, insurance brokers, and financial advisers. I thought the talk went great, but I was startled to find out later that my audience didn't care for it. In fact, they thought it stunk.

Worse yet, I learned this discouraging fact only two days before I planned to give the same talk to an even more challenging audience of accountants. I started to panic, but I quickly got myself back on track and analyzed the situation. I realized that there was nothing wrong with my talk; instead, the problem lay in the setting. After a morning of nuts-and-bolts presentations, my audience was primed for more of the same, and I'd asked them to make too big a mental leap.

So I began my talk to the second audience by saying this: "A funny thing happened to me on the way to this talk. I learned a couple of days ago that this exact same talk received an awful rating from an easier audience than you." (This generated a few surprised and nervous chuckles, but created enough intrigue to keep them listening.) I went on, "I realized that it wasn't the talk but the setting. So I'd like to try something that will help you get something valuable from what I'm going to say, rather than being disappointed."

To help them make the mental transition from the technical talks they'd heard all morning to my transformational talk, I asked them to think about some life-changing moments. For instance, I asked them to imagine it was the weekend after September 11, 2001, and they were in their house of worship and needed to hear something calming and reassuring because they knew their lives had changed forever—or to imagine that a child they loved, who had a learning disability and wasn't expected to make it through high school, had just graduated from college.

I could sense their minds moving from *what new tax laws should I be up on?* to *what really matters in my life?*. As I looked out across the room, I saw hundreds of people beginning to focus intently and expectantly on what I'd say next.

A few days later, the meeting planner e-mailed to tell me my talk was by far the best received talk of the day. Several people, she said, told her it was the best talk they'd ever heard. By baring my weaknesses to my audience, I'd created an empathy that allowed them to understand and appreciate my message. And in figuring out my mistake and overcoming it, I learned some key skills that made me a much better and more confident speaker.

➤ Usable Insight

Show poise by openly expressing the misgivings people have about you, and they'll be more likely to give you their positive and undivided attention.

➤ Action Step

If you know that something about you makes other people uncomfortable, practice ways to describe what the problem is and how other people can respond to it. Rehearse in front of a mirror until you are sure you can do this comfortably in public.

19

FROM TRANSACTION TO TRANSFORMATION

Benefit: Move a person from considering to "willing to do" by transforming a relationship from impersonal to personal.

They don't see the sky.
—AFRICAN NATIVE WALKING THROUGH MANHATTAN

M y daughter, preparing to interview with a senior manager at a Wall Street financial firm, asked me, "What question could I ask that would help me stand out from the crowd?"

An hour and a half later, she beeped me in the middle of a meeting and excitedly said, "Dad, I asked him the question you suggested, and he reacted exactly like you said he would. He glanced up toward the ceiling for a moment and said, 'That's a great question and something I don't have an answer to, but should.' He really connected with me after that."

Here's what my daughter said to earn this interviewer's interest. When he asked her if she had a question, she responded with this:

"I'd like you to imagine it's a year from now, and you and your bosses are reviewing the people you've hired this year—and when it comes to this position, they say, 'Get us 10 more like that one. That person was one of the best hires we've had in a long time.' Can you tell me what that person did for them and you to get such a rave review?"

I knew the question would work. I also told my daughter how she'd know it worked: by watching the interviewer's eyes. Because at the moment he glanced up and away, she'd know she'd moved him from transaction to transformation.

■ NEGOTIATING VERSUS RELATING

These days, we don't relate—we transact. Lovers and married couples negotiate everything from dinner to vacations to sex. Parents negotiate with kids about getting ready for school and doing their homework. Managers negotiate when they're not coercing. Everyone's into "What will you do for me?" and "What do I need to do in return?"

Transacting is fine if your goal is to exchange information or negotiate contracts, but it has a fatal flaw: it doesn't open the mind or the heart. A transactional communication is like an encounter with your ATM. Money comes out of your bank account, money goes into your hand, and everything's utterly fair—but you don't feel like saying "Gosh, thanks!" when it's over.

Transactional communications don't create traction in a relationship because they're impersonal and shallow. These exchanges won't necessarily drive people away—my daughter could have asked her interviewer, "What are the health benefits that come with the job?" without upsetting the person—but they won't draw people closer either. Like the ATM transaction, they're rarely life-changing events, and they're "all about you" instead of "all about the other person or company."

To create such a life-changing event, you need to move beyond transacting to relating. How? By asking questions that let the other person tell you: "This is what I think," "This is who I am," "This is what I want to achieve," or "This is how you can play a part in making my life better."

Years ago, for instance, I realized that most of the CEOs and managers I meet are not just smart but also wise—but they don't often get a chance to share their wisdom. They're focused so intently on the mundane day-to-day problems of running a business that they rarely have the opportunity to think deeply and creatively and use their highest and usually considerable intellectual abilities. That creates frustration, even if it's on an unconscious level.

When I ask these people questions that let them open their minds and express their intelligence, I witness a peculiar phenomenon: These hurried professionals, whose most valuable resource is time, hunger to spend more of that time with me. Nearly a third of the time they tell their assistants to hold all calls, go over the allotted time with me, walk me from their corner offices to the entrance of their company to have more time with me, or say to me: "Darn it Mark, please remind me that we run out of time whenever we meet, so we can schedule more time or meet for dinner."

I get this response for a simple reason: I'm satisfying the mirror neuron gap I talked about in Chapter 2. These people work hard and do their best, and they want the world to acknowledge that they're intelligent, valuable, and creative. But rather than receiving acknowledgment and appreciation for their ideas and talent, they typically hear "The board won't like those numbers" or "Where's the cost analysis?" or "Your department's late with the monthly report." This makes them feel like little more than cogs in the wheel.

I'm truly fascinated by these people as human beings, not just cogs, and I let them know it—often with a single question. The result, typically, is active consideration or even immediate buy-in to what I'm saying.

For instance, a while back, I met with Bill, the senior vice president of a software company. We talked at some length about the reason for our meeting, ostensibly to deal with a personnel problem at his firm. Bill, clearly an intelligent and interesting guy, was firmly in transacting mode: When are you available? How long will you need? How much is this going to cost?

After a half-hour or so of this, I said to Bill: "To help me better understand if and how I can help you, tell me what your company and specifically your department is trying to accomplish that's critical and important, and why your company selected that goal."

Bill paused, looked up to the ceiling for a few moments, and replied: "That's a very good question, and I'll need to think about it more."

At that point, I could feel our relationship moving to a higher level. In a manner of speaking, Bill "saw the sky." He stepped outside the little world of bargaining and strategizing and quid-pro-quos and thought about the big picture for his company and his own future. By allowing him to do that I created a connection with him, and when his eyes met mine again, our conversation was no longer a negotiation but a dialogue.

The key to crafting a transformational question is simple: Ask yourself, "What single question will show this person that I'm interested in his or her ideas, interests, future success, or life?" Then ask it. Here are some examples.

- "If you could change one thing about the direction of your company, what would it be?"
- "If there is one thing I can do to help you move more quickly toward your goals, what would it be?"
- "What's the one thing you're proudest of accomplishing?"

To see why questions like these have a more powerful effect than transactional questions, let's look at two different scenarios. Both involve Noemi, who's starting her first day at a new job, and her boss. Here's the first.

> **Boss:** Hi Noemi, how's it going?
>
> **Noemi:** Great, thanks. I appreciate your assistant's help. The first day is always a little confusing, but I'm getting the hang of things.
>
> **Boss:** Great. If you have any questions, just talk with my assistant.
>
> **Noemi:** Okay, thanks. Oh, and do you know where I can get a stapler?
>
> **Boss:** Sure, just check the supply closet. And can you get me the Johnson files by tonight?

There's nothing wrong with this conversation, but Noemi is making zero impression on her boss right now. If he remembers anything at all about her later on, it'll be the stapler.

Now, picture the impression she'll make with this conversation.

BOSS: Hi Noemi, how's it going?

NOEMI: Great, thanks. I appreciate your assistant's help. Oh, and before you go, do you have a second for two quick questions?

BOSS: Um, sure. What are they?

NOEMI: Just to make sure I get off on the right foot—what are three things you'd like me to *always* do, and three things you'd like me to *never* do?

BOSS: Um. Wow. (Looking up and away.) Interesting question. I may have to think about it and get back to you. But right off the top of my head, I'd say never try to cover up a problem—just tell me up front about it, so I don't get blindsided. And [laughing] always put my wife through, even if I'm on another line. Otherwise, I'll hear about it when I get home. Oh—and you know Leo, who's going to be working with you on the Bradley account? I know you millennials tend to treat Boomers as old timers, but he's the best person on my team, so pay a lot of attention to what he has to say.

The questions Noemi asks her boss in the second scenario are simple ones—much simpler than "What do you want to do with your life?" or "What direction do you want your company to take?" But they accomplish a similar goal: They take the conversation out of transactional mode (Where's my stapler?/Can you get me the files?) and move it to a higher plane (What's important to you? How can I help?).

The boss who hears Noemi's questions will stop and think, and when he makes eye contact with her again, he'll be seeing her in a new light. From that point on, she'll be a colleague—not just somebody who needs a stapler.

■ HOW'S THIS FOR A SALES PITCH? ■

I often speak to sales and marketing teams at pharmaceutical companies, including Eli Lilly, Astra Zenica, and Bristol Myers Squibb, at off-sites, but I also enjoy helping drug sales reps who visit me in my capacity as a clinical psychiatrist. (I maintain a small clinical psychiatric practice, just to get the free samples. Just joking. . . . C'mon, lighten up.)

I tell them what would work to get through to me, and they use this information successfully to get through to other physicians. First, I explain that most physicians work harder today to make the same amount of money they made 10 years ago, all the time watching other people with fewer years of training make much more money and have more financial security.

I also tell them that most physicians feel that they take care of everyone—family, aging parents, front office staff—while many feel, but don't dwell on the fact, that nobody takes care of them. (Talk about a huge mirror neuron gap!) In fact, many will say that the best way to care about them is to not add any more responsibilities to their plate.

Also, by the nature of their practices, physicians are almost completely transactional—"Tell me your symptom, let me examine you for signs and test you for lab results, and I'll come up with a diagnosis and treatment plan. . . . Next?"

So if a sales rep wants to shift to a transformational and more memorable conversation, I tell the rep to say the following to the physician at the end of a sales presentation: "Excuse me, Dr. X, do you have a couple minutes for me to ask you a different question?"

Most doctors will be annoyed, thinking the salesperson is going to hit on them for free medical advice, but out of civility will say, "Go ahead."

Then I tell the rep to follow with: "I've heard from many physicians that it's not as much fun as it used to be and that they have to work longer and harder just to keep up. You guys work so hard, I just wanted to know if it's still fun for you to be a doctor."

The sales reps who report back tell me that most doctors are completely caught off guard and disarmed, and then look up to reflect and respond with: "You know, it is harder being a doctor, and I'm not sure I would recommend it to my children, but it's still fun. Almost every day, I get to make a difference in a patient's life and when I see the relief I can give someone, it still gives me a lift."

Sometimes a doctor even says "thank you," and it nearly always makes the reps memorable. And if these reps' medications are as good as their competitors', these doctors will often give the reps' products a try.

So if you're a pharmaceutical company rep, here's the formula you want to remember: Caring = More Rx's written. Not a bad ROI (Return On a little more Investment of time).

■ WHAT QUESTION WOULD MAKE *YOU* LOOK UP?

One great thing about the "eyes-to-the-sky" technique is that you can use it to reach even the most difficult person you communicate with: yourself. Did you ever stop to think about how much of your internal conversation is transactional? If you're like most people, your inner monologue goes something like this: *If I eat this dough-nut, I'll need to spend more time at the gym. Jeez, I'm late, and Sally will be mad at me. Too bad, she was late last time, so I'm probably okay. Damn, I didn't get the taxes done yet. I'll need to stay up late. I should be spending more time with the kids. . . .*

The next time you catch yourself running on that transactional hamster wheel, try something different. Stop what you're doing, and sit down. Take a breath. And say to yourself: "What would I like to be doing with my life this time next year?" or "What do I need more or less of in my life right now?" or "If my kids looked at me 20 years from now, what would make them proud of me?"

Ask the right question of yourself, and you'll find your eyes moving up—a clear sign that your mind is opening up to new possibilities. Answer your own question ("I'd like to be spending more time with my family," "I need to spend less time in point-less meetings," "I want my kids to be proud that I took chances instead of always playing it safe") and you'll deepen your relationship with the most important person in your life: the person in the mirror.

➡ *Usable Insight*
Cause people to look up and reflect on what you've asked them,

and when they look back down at you, the conversation will never be the same again. . . . It'll be better.

➡ *Action Step*
The next time you're stuck in one of those transactional conversational ruts with a partner or family member—say, arguing over who's going to do the laundry or take out the trash—stop, smile, and say: "What's something fun or important that you think you and I should do within the next five years?" Then see how fast you move from "It's your turn to do dishes" to a new and better life plan.

20

SIDE BY SIDE

*Benefit: Lower another person's guard
and move the person from resistance to listening.*

A preaching point is not a meeting point.
—MOTHER TERESA, FOUNDER OF THE
MISSIONS OF CHARITY IN CALCUTTA

It's the weekend, and Will and his 15-year-old son, Evan, are driving to the sporting goods store. Evan is hoping to make his school's archery team, and Will's taking him to pick out some new arrows.

Evan, uncommunicative as only a teenager can be, taps his foot to the music on his iPod. As they drive, Will talks idly about stuff at home and at work. He throws out some ideas for the family's upcoming vacation, thinks out loud about grilling some steaks when they get home, and then talks a little about one of his coworkers who's making problems for everybody.

The guy, Will says, has always been a pain in the butt, and everybody knew he'd screw up eventually. Then he says casually, "Tell me, which of your friends do you think is most likely to get into big trouble some day?"

"Huh?" says Evan, taken by surprise. He's not thrilled with having to field a question, but it sounds better than the usual "Are you bringing up your Spanish grade?" or "We need to talk about that orange hair."

"Yeah," Will continues, "I was just wondering which of your friends takes too many chances and will probably get into major problems sometime—and, more importantly, what makes you think it will be that particular person?"

Caught off-guard by the fact that his dad is soliciting his opinion, Evan considers the question. Then he responds, in an unusually cooperative fashion, "I think it'll be Jake, because once he gets on a roll, nobody can stop him, and he's already messed up a couple times."

"Really," Will responds, resisting the temptation to offer unsolicited advice or input and instead keeping the conversation going.

"Yeah, he already did a couple of things that got him grounded. I don't think he and his parents get along real well," Evan continues.

"Well, I guess it will be interesting to see if your prediction comes true. By the way, if he gets in trouble, what will you probably do?" Will adds.

"Geez, I don't know," Evan says. He thinks about it for a minute. "I guess since I'm his friend, I'll try and help him out somehow and probably try to keep him from doing it again."

"He's lucky to have you as a friend," Will concludes.

"Yeah, I guess I'm pretty okay in that department," Evan finishes.

So . . . what was that all about?

Will is getting his son to open up to him by using a technique I call Side by Side. It's based on the following three facts.

■ Sitting people down and lecturing them rarely works, because it makes them defensive—and when they're defensive, they hide things from you. Work side by side with them in a cooperative activity, however, and you'll lower their guard and get them to open up. That's why hostage negotiators try to get hostage takers to commit to a shared activity, such as allowing food or medical supplies into a building. It's also why the elders at an Amish barn-raising or quilting bee uncover more deep secrets than a spy in bed with a drunken politician.

■ Questioning works better than telling. That's why Will didn't *tell* Evan, "Don't let your friends get you into trouble." Instead, he asked questions that made Evan think, "Who's likely to get into trouble, and what should I do if it happens?" In other words, Will didn't talk down to Evan, or talk at him. Instead, the two talked side by side *emotionally* as well as physically.

■ When you allow one revelation to lead to another without getting in the way, you learn even more. So rather than doing a "bait and switch" by luring his son into a conversation that ended with a lecture ("Well, you'd better avoid Jake, or he'll get you into trouble too"), Will employed a conversation deepener ("Really") and a second question that enabled Evan to share even more.

These elements of the Side-by-Side approach—asking questions during a shared moment, and then deepening the conversation with more questions—are as powerful as communication gets: so powerful that they form the core of the Socratic Method. Socrates never told anybody anything; he just walked around town with people asking them questions until they figured out the answers themselves, and in the process he helped create Western civilization.

However, this technique isn't just for parents or philosophers. It's also the basis for the effectiveness of MBWA (managing by walking around), a management technique that's been used successfully for decades. It's an outstanding tool for accomplishing two goals: finding out what's really going on in your area, and creating affinity with coworkers in the process.

> One advantage of the Side-by-Side technique is that it doesn't focus on things a person did wrong in the past. Instead, you can use it to explore ways to make things go right in the future—just as Will did when he asked Evan what he'd do if his friend got in trouble. So instead of delving into a person's past screw-ups, you give the person a chance to avoid future ones.

The Side-by-Side approach is simple: join the other person in an activity (preferably one in which you can be helpful—but even eating lunch together is good), and then ask questions designed to gain insight into what the person is doing, thinking, and feeling. Here's an example.

> GRAHAM (NOTICING VICTORIA, A SUBORDINATE, PREPARING INFOR-MATION PACKETS FOR A CLIENT MEETING): Wow, that's a big pile of paperwork you're handling. Here, hand me some of those folders —I've got some free time, and I'll be glad to help out.
>
> VICTORIA: Thanks. I appreciate it.
>
> GRAHAM (AFTER A FEW MINUTES OF HELPING): So, what do you think about this material we're giving the clients?
>
> VICTORIA: I hadn't really thought about it. I guess now that you mention it, it seems like a lot of stuff for them to wade through.
>
> GRAHAM: What's your impression of how useful it is?
>
> VICTORIA: Well, it seems like when clients talk to us on the phone, they want to know if the new system is easy to learn and if the training is quick. I'm not sure they want to know all this complicated information about the new technology. They just want to know how fast they can integrate it.
>
> GRAHAM: What other thoughts are you picking up from clients?
>
> VICTORIA: I know sometimes they're a little confused by our doc-umentation. Maybe we should look at simplifying it. . . .

The Side-by-Side technique is easy to use, but it comes with three cautions. The biggest one is: When you get people to lower their guard, don't violate their trust. Do *not* use this technique to troll for negative information, or people will feel like you're trying to spy on them or trap them rather than trying to learn from them. Accept negative information with grace, but don't seek it out.

Also, don't argue with the person you're talking with. If he or she says something you disagree with, resist the urge to explain why you're right. Instead, deepen the conversation by asking another question. Here's an example,

> SUE (MIGUEL'S MANAGER): Hey, looks like the new company news-letter is almost done. Wow, it looks great—super job. Want me to help with the proofing?

MIGUEL: Sure. I'm glad you like it. But I'm not totally happy about it, because I don't think the new administrative building should be the lead story.

SUE: What is it about the story you don't like?

MIGUEL: It's boring. Nobody cares except the boss. He's the one who insisted on it.

SUE: What would you like to see in the next issue?

MIGUEL: Something the employees care about, not just the boss.

SUE: What do you think would interest them?

MIGUEL: More stuff about the changes in the vacation policy. I had three people ask me just today if they can get more information about that. Some of them think the new policy is unfair to long-term employees, and they want to know why the company decided to make the changes.

Note that when Miguel criticizes the boss's idea, Sue doesn't say, "Well, he's the boss, so he gets to make the decisions"—a complete conversation stopper. And she doesn't argue ("Hey, lots of people want to know what the new building's going to look like"), which would alienate him. Instead, she lets him go deeper—and in the process, she uncovers an issue affecting company morale.

And that brings me to my third caution: When you ask people questions, respect their answers. If they offer a good idea, act on it (and let them know that you did). Even if they're off base, acknowledge their remarks with a comment like, "That's worth thinking about" or "I hadn't looked at it that way." If the situation warrants, acknowledge a comment by saying "Smart idea" or "I'm glad you're on our team—I need people with creative ideas like that."

If you're a manager or CEO, use the Side-by-Side approach on a regular basis, and you'll see a variety of results. You'll nip toxic rumors in the bud. Employers who started out as strangers will warm up to you. And you'll do your own job faster, better, and more easily because you'll gain a deeper understanding of the people around you.

■ "What Would You Say. . . ." ■

I was a second-year psychiatry resident at UCLA, and a nurse on the oncology floor was responding to my question: "What has Mrs. Franklin been saying and doing since the MRI showed that her breast cancer is back?"

"She's been crying a lot and her family and her oncologist are trying to reassure her that it's still treatable," the nurse replied.

I continued: "In your experience, what works best in these situations?"

Jane, Mrs. Franklin's lead nurse, joined in, offering: "The more we allow people to have their feelings and become sad or angry, the quicker it passes. Some of the younger oncologists get uncomfortable with their patients' emotions and their anxiety throws a monkey wrench in the works."

Rather than making the new-doctor mistake of trying to sound like I knew it all, I asked, "Jane you're obviously very experienced about this. What could you say to those doctors to help them and help the patient get through the bad news easier?"

"Hmm," Jane thought. "I could tell the doctors that I know they care, but it might go smoother if they allow their patients to have a strong initial reaction after hearing bad news. It's helpful to tell them, 'I understand you're upset—do you have any questions now? Otherwise I'll give you a little time to adjust to the news and be back in a couple hours to check back with you and we can talk more about it then.'"

"That's a great plan," I said gratefully. "Jane, you really know your stuff and really care about the patients *and* the doctors. I'll check back tomorrow, and you can fill me in on how it went."

Not only did this Side-by-Side interaction solve one of the problems I had been called to handle—it did so without my having to write up one of the dreaded formal consultation reports that we residents hated.

As a result of my "consulting by walking around," I wound up doing nearly the most consultations *and* the fewest written formal consultations of all the psychiatric residents assigned to the consultation service during my six-month stint. More important, writing up fewer consultations enabled me to spend more time face-to-face with the cancer patients I was there to help.

➡ *Usable Insight*
When you can't get through face to face, try side by side.

➡ *Action Step*
If you're a manager, use the Side-by-Side technique to find out what's going on with your most productive employee and see if you can uncover ways to make that person even happier about working for you. Then turn around and use it with your least productive employee, and see if you can discover any clues about why the person underperforms.

21

FILL IN THE BLANKS

Benefit: Move a person to the "willing to do"
stage by making the person feel felt and understood.

To listen well is as powerful a means
of communication and influence as to talk well.
—JOHN MARSHALL, CHIEF JUSTICE
OF THE SUPREME COURT, 1801–1835

K ate is thinking about hiring me to stop the hemorrhaging of star players from her company in the aftermath of an ugly partnership split up. But she's not sure she trusts me, and she's not quite ready to bare her company's flaws to a stranger.

After we say hello, Kate crosses her arms and waits for me to ask the questions every other consultant asks: "What results are you looking for?" "What's your time frame?" "How much are you willing to spend?"

But I don't. Instead, I say: "You're thinking of hiring someone like me because you want to _____," accompanying my words with an inviting hand gesture to encourage her to respond. Then I sit quietly and listen. And wait.

After a pause, Kate uncrosses her arms, leans forward, and says, "Because I want to make this a good place to work again. And I want people to work for me because they want to, not because they have to."

> At that point, I know I can help Kate . . . and I'm also pretty sure she'll let me. That's because I've created traction by pulling Kate to me, rather than pushing myself on her.

When you and a prospective customer or client first meet, the playing field is level. As soon as you sell or try to convince the other person of anything, the power shifts to the client. The key is to keep clients pursuing you right out of the gate.

The secret to this is to invite these people into a conversation rather than asking questions that put them on the defensive—and that's where the Fill-in-the-Blanks approach comes in.

When you ask direct questions, you're hoping to communicate a sincere interest. The people on the receiving end of your questions, however, can feel challenged, like a schoolchild being put on the spot by a teacher or coach. Sensitive questions posed at the right times can powerfully transform a relationship (see Chapters 6 and 19), but hitting a new client with a transactional question like "What do you want?" or "Can I show you why our product is better?" can create immediate resistance.

The Fill-in-the-Blanks approach has the opposite effect: it draws a person toward you. You don't come off as a demanding teacher or coach; instead, you sound like a trusted uncle, aunt, grandfather, or grandmother who's saying: "C'mon. Let's talk this out and find a solution."

Try this yourself, and see if you sense the difference between the two techniques. First, picture me sitting across from you and saying, "So, what do you expect to get from this book?" A little intimidating, isn't it? Now picture me saying in an encouraging way, "You're reading this book because you want to learn how to _____ . And the reason it's important for you to learn how to do that now is _____. And if you could learn that and put it into action now, it would benefit you by _____." If you're like most people, you'll feel willing and in fact a little eager to open up and share your thoughts with me.

Asking people to fill in the blanks also eliminates the threat of dissonance. If you make the wrong assumption about a person's needs or motives—for instance, thinking Mr. Jones is looking for "simple and cheap" when he really needs "fast and efficient"—you can lose a client or a sale. Let your client fill in the blanks, and you'll have the right answers.

The Fill-in-the-Blanks approach works especially well in sales, where it catches people off guard because they're braced for a hard sell. When you surprise them by doing something totally different, their barriers often fall quickly. This approach also figuratively and actually disarms people, because when you combine your words with an inviting hand gesture it typically causes people to uncross their arms and open their minds. Here's an example.

> DANA: Hi, thanks so much for taking the time to meet with me.
>
> SANDHYA: You're welcome. But I'm in a big hurry, and I'm really not sure we're interested in your software right now. So can we do this fast?
>
> DANA: Yes, and thanks for working me in when you're so busy. Your assistant mentioned when I got here that you're up against a big deadline.
>
> SANDHYA: A life-or-death deadline, as a matter of fact. But I have about 15 minutes.
>
> DANA: I appreciate it, and I'll make sure we're done on time. To start, I'm hoping to get a little information: You're thinking of buying our software, or a product like it, because *(gesturing invitingly with her hand)* _____.
>
> SANDHYA: Well . . . because our current software isn't doing the job for us. It drives us crazy because it crashes too often—and it's way too slow. In fact, it's one of the reasons we're in such a panic about meeting this deadline now.
>
> DANA: And by changing to our software or someone else's, you're hoping to accomplish _____.
>
> SANDHYA: More work! We need to be doing more in less time, and we can't do that if the system crashes once or twice a week. That's just unacceptable.

Voila!: instant traction. In fact, Sandhya's actually doing a large part of Dana's sales job for her by reviewing all the reasons why her company desperately needs new software. If Dana's product truly is better, her odds of making a sale are looking good—even though she hasn't said a single word about herself or her product yet.

Incidentally, Dana does two other smart things in her opening move that you should emulate. The first is to say "you're thinking of buying . . ." because that's more positive than "you're trying to find," which sounds like hard work, or "you need," which implies a subservient position. "Thinking of buying" reinforces people's belief that they're in control and have positive options and choices.

Dana also talks about "our software or a product like it," rather than just saying "our product." (As a consultant, I use the words "me or someone like me.") Acknowledging that a person can choose someone else or a different product makes a potential client feel less hit upon or cornered.

But the real force of the Fill-in-the-Blanks technique lies in the simple fact that you don't tell people what they want or even ask them what they want. Instead, you get *them* to tell *you* what they want. This immediately makes people think, "Yes, yes—that's why I'm here meeting with you." As a result, you don't need to put your foot in the door. Instead, the client or customer will open it for you, and invite you in.

■ THE NEVER AGAIN TOOL ■

Here's a very different use for the Fill-in-the-Blanks technique: Use it to get through to yourself.

Just like everybody else (including me), you sometimes do excruciatingly dumb things. That's not a big deal, unless you keep doing these same things over and over again.

If you ever find yourself trapped in a cycle of self-defeating behavior, break that cycle with a Fill-in-the-Blanks variant I call the Never Again Tool. It's an excellent way to lower your own defenses and start an inner dialogue that can save you lots of trouble in the future.

To understand why, think about your typical response after you commit an impulsive or foolish act that hurts your career or infuriates your loved ones. Most likely, you say to yourself: "What a dumb ass! What a moron! I can't believe how stupid you are. Stupid, stupid, stupid. Can you be any more stupid?" Or you say to yourself: "Hey, it wasn't *my* fault. I can't help it if our clients are jerks/the boss is an idiot who didn't support me/my partner makes me lose my temper when she's too critical."

Neither of these reactions does you any good (although both are perfectly normal in those first horrible seconds when you realize you've messed up). If you don't move quickly beyond these knee-jerk responses, you'll set yourself up for future failure by convincing yourself either that (a) you're an idiot who'll keep screwing up or (b) the people around you are idiots who make you screw up and there's nothing you can do about it.

Instead of laying the groundwork for your next disaster, do something different the next time you make a mistake. Take out an index card, write down the following words, and fill in the blanks with your answers:

1. If I had *that* to do over again, what I would do differently is:

   _____

   _____.

2. I would do things differently because:

   _____

   _____.

3. My commitment to do this (the new action) the next time is_____.
   (1 = won't do it; 5 = maybe; 10 = *will* do it).

4. A good person to hold me accountable for doing this would be:

   _____

   _____.

This is a powerful approach because you're not wallowing in self-blame or deflecting responsibility onto someone else—two traps that allow you to avoid looking honestly at what really happened and why. Instead, you're reframing your experience in a way that leads to positive action.

When you do this exercise, be sure to fill in that last blank by selecting a mentor who'll keep you honest. Pick someone you trust and respect, and whose respect you desire in return. This is an excellent way to make yourself stop and think when you're on the brink of repeating a big mistake.

➡ *Usable Insight*

Direct questions make people think you're talking *at* them. Let them fill in the blanks, and they'll feel you're talking *with* them.

➡ *Action Step*

A big problem for many managers (especially women) is that they have trouble saying "no" to any request—even if their plates are already full. That's because they're responsible problem-solvers and they're hard-wired to want to help. And that's where filling in your own blank using the Never Again Tool can come in handy.

The problem is that saying "yes" too often leads to burnout, and it tends to make everyone unhappy if you're spread too thin. If you keep saying "yes" when you need to say "I'm sorry, I'll have to pass," try the Never Again Tool on yourself. When it's time to pick someone to hold you accountable, pick a partner or child who's tired of having to fight for your attention.

22

TAKE IT ALL THE WAY TO "NO"

Benefit: Move a person rapidly through every phase of the Persuasion Cycle from resistance to "doing," by creating agreement where none exists.

Life is a series of sales situations,
and the answer is "no" if you don't ask.
—PATRICIA FRIPP, EXECUTIVE SPEECH COACH

Walter Dunn was one of the top people at Coca-Cola for four decades. Dunn was responsible for getting Coke many major accounts, including Disney and several professional sports organizations.

Walter told me how years ago he tried to get Coke into one of the main movie theater chains. After speaking with the theater representative for a while, he got this response: "Sorry, Walter, the answer is 'No.' We've decided to go with Pepsi."

Without missing a beat, Walter replied: "What question did I fail to ask, or what problem did I fail to address, that—if I had—would have caused you to give me a different answer?"

The man from the theater chain responded: "Pepsi knew we ̶ vating our lobbies and offered to underwrite a big ̶ hat."

̶ ould do that too," Walter added.

̶ you've got the account," the theater representative

Ask managers or salespeople, "What's the biggest mistake you can make?" and often they'll say, "Asking for too much."

But they're wrong—because in reality, the biggest mistake you can make is to ask for too little. When you ask for too little, you'll have some explaining to do when your higher-ups ask why you didn't get more.

A better approach is to keep pushing for what you want until you receive a "no." This will tell you that you're in range of getting the most that's possible from the other person. More important, it will be one of your best opportunities to demonstrate poise and close a sale or a deal.

Most people are scared to try this approach, because they think "no" really means "no." In dating, it most definitely does—but in business, surprisingly often, it doesn't. To get from "no" to "yes," however, you need to make the right moves. Here's what to do.

Let's say you're trying to get a client (we'll call him Ned) to buy a product, hire you as a consultant, or retain your firm for a project. But after you lay out the deal you're hoping for, Ned says no.

When Ned does this, he's feeling a little edgy and defensive because he expects you to be frustrated or angry or upset—or to start in with a hard sell, making his life hell for the next 15 minutes. If you do any of these things, you're not going to win Ned over. Instead, take a breath and then, as earnestly as possible, say something like this: "I either pushed too hard or failed to address something that was important to you, didn't I?"

After Ned recovers from his momentary shock at your self-awareness and humility, he'll nod in agreement or even say, with an awkward smile, "You sure did." At that moment, the advantage shifts to you. Why? Because Ned's mentally agreeing and aligning himself psychologically with you. In other words, without knowing it, he's actually beginning to say "yes."

Once you score this agreement ("Yes, I agree that you blew it!"), it's time to use the Fill in the Blanks approach from Chapter 21 to build on the moment by saying, "And the point where I went too far and the deal points I failed to address were _____."

If Ned's like most people, he'll respond honestly to these questions. As he elaborates on his points, he'll do two things: He'll get his frustration at you off his chest, and he'll tell you what he needs from you. Both of these will give you the power to go from "No" to "Yes."

Here's a good example of how this technique works. It involves Luke, an account manager at a public relations firm. Luke is setting his sights on a big win: He wants to persuade Joel, a CEO, to leave a long-term relationship with his current PR firm and switch to Luke's firm for a major campaign.

> JOEL: I'm sorry. We're pretty happy with what we have now, and you're just not quite the right match for us. But I really appreciate your time.
>
> LUKE: I'm very grateful for your time as well. And could I ask you just one thing?
>
> JOEL: (a little defensive): Okay, but I really don't want to argue about my decision.
>
> LUKE: No, it's nothing like that. I'm just wondering if you could tell me—the question I failed to ask or the issue I didn't address that would have made you feel differently was _____.
>
> JOEL: Well . . . actually. I just think the other agency is a better fit because they have a staff member who actually worked in our industry for a little while, and it doesn't sound like you do.
>
> LUKE: You know, I should have addressed that. One thing we often do is bring in consultants with extensive experience in a client's field. We did that last year with the Chandler account, because they wanted us to be able to hit the ground running. That was a big project so we actually brought two consultants on board who had 40 years of experience in agriculture between them.
>
> JOEL: Really?
>
> LUKE: Sure. Chandler was thrilled with its campaign, and gives us full credit for its jump in profits this year. So that's just one example of what we can do with expert consultants. Our firm is only satisfied with extraordinary results that exceed our clients' expectations, because our reputation depends on it. We know our strengths and, when we need expertise in other areas, we tap into outside people who are excellent in those areas. So, the

results for our clients are always top notch. In your case, we have an outstanding recruiting team whose members can quickly identify the perfect people to provide us with industry experience so we can achieve the best results for you. Because of our reputation, we can attract the best talent in any field.

JOEL (STARTING TO MOVE FROM "NO" TO "YES"): Won't that bump up the cost a lot?

LUKE: Even if we bring in an expert consultant—someone with more experience than your current agency is providing—we'll still be less expensive because of the money we save with our in-house production capabilities. And since we use only people who will deliver excellent results, we avoid needless time and expense down the road because there won't be any need to fix a flawed campaign.

JOEL: Hmmm. . . .

The great thing about this approach is that the client feels in control—and *is* in control—the entire time. You're not whining or browbeating or otherwise trying to overpower the person; instead, you're letting the person freely offer the information you need to make a power play.

And yes, this is a slightly risky thing to do, and maybe not something to try if you're a brand-new account manager or junior salesperson. It's also an approach to avoid if you're content with making safe, low-level deals. But if you have confidence and you're willing to move outside your comfort zone, give it a shot—because otherwise you'll never know just how great you can be at clinching the big deals. Just ask Walter Dunn.

 Usable Insight
Until someone says "no" to you, you're not asking for enough.

 Action Step
If you're in sales or management, think of the last sale or deal you made. Now take a piece of paper and write the answer to this question: "What more could I have asked for, and possibly gotten, if I hadn't been scared of hearing "no"?

23

THE POWER THANK YOU
AND POWER APOLOGY

*Benefit: Move a person from "doing" to "glad they did"
and "continuing to do" by using the Power Thank You,
or from resistance to listening with the Power Apology.*

Nine-tenths of wisdom is appreciation.
—DALE DAUTEN, NEWSPAPER COLUMNIST

I 've learned more about life from my children than I
ever did from my psychiatry training—especially when
it comes to touching other people's hearts and minds.
For instance, I learned from my daughter Lauren that a single gesture can warm another person's heart for years. In her case, the gesture was a note she e-mailed me when she was 23 years old. It says:

> Hi Dad, Last night I was walking around Manhattan as I often
> do with my friends talking about how confused we felt about our
> futures. And as often happens I said, "My dad said . . ." and as
> always happens, it made the conversation considerably better. I
> don't know how many of my friends can say the same about their
> fathers. I am so lucky to have such a wise dad, even if he does live
> 3,000 miles away. See you in a few weeks. Love, Lauren.

I wouldn't sell that note for a million bucks. And no matter how
bad a day is, or how rude or annoying people are to me, or how lit-

tle positive feedback I receive, I know that I matter—because there's a piece of paper I carry in my wallet that says so.

■ "THANK YOU" VERSUS THE POWER THANK YOU

I have wonderful kids, and they're great about offering thanks when I do stuff for them. But Lauren's note stood out because it wasn't just a thank you—it was a Power Thank You.

Clearly, there's nothing wrong with simply saying "thanks" when someone helps you out. In fact, that's usually the right thing to do. But if you stop there, your communication is merely transactional (you did something nice for me, so I'll say something polite to you). It doesn't touch the other person or strengthen the relationship between you.

That's why if you're deeply grateful to someone who's done an exceptional favor for you, you need to express that emotion by going beyond the plain words "thank you" and instead offer a Power Thank You. When you do this, your words will generate strong feelings of gratitude, respect, and affinity in the other person.

Here's my favorite version of the Power Thank You. It was inspired by Heidi Wall, filmmaker and co-founder of the Flash Forward Institute, and it has three parts:

Part 1: Thank the person for something specific that he or she did for you. (It can also be something the person refrained from doing that would have hurt you.)

Part 2: Acknowledge the effort it took for the person to help you by saying something like: "I know you didn't have to do _____" or "I know you went out of your way to do_____."

Part 3: Tell the person the difference that his or her act personally made to you.

Here's an example of the Power Thank You in action.

DONNA, A MANAGER, SPEAKING TO A SUBORDINATE: Larry, do you have a sec?

LARRY: Sure. What's up?

> DONNA: Nothing. I just wanted to take a minute to thank you for handling the Bennett account so well when I was out of the office for my emergency surgery.
>
> LARRY: Hey, no problem. I was glad to help.
>
> DONNA: Actually, I'm sure it *did* create some problems for you. I know you were counting on taking your kids to the soccer semi-finals and I heard from your coworkers that instead you spent the whole weekend in the office boning up on the details of the account. I don't think many people would have rearranged their schedules so willingly—and I doubt that most people could carry off a meeting with Bennett as brilliantly as you did.
>
> LARRY: Well, thanks. I was a little worried about it all, but I'm glad we pulled it off.
>
> DONNA: Don't kid yourself. *You* pulled it off. You made both of us look good, and you made a big score for the whole department. I'm very grateful, and so is the rest of the team.

Donna could have simply said "thanks" in this situation, and that's what most managers would do. If she had, however, Larry—although he's an awfully nice guy—would have felt a little cheated. Why? If a person performs an extraordinary act of kindness or assistance and all you say is "thanks," you create a mirror neuron gap (more about this in Chapter 2) because emotionally you're not giving back as much as you received. Saying "thanks" is better than nothing, but it's not good enough.

Donna's Power Thank You, however, made Larry feel totally mirrored. She didn't just express appreciation; she also acknowledged Larry's kindness, intelligence, commitment, and willingness to make a sacrifice to help other people. As a result, she strengthened her bond with Larry and gave him even more incentive to come through in tough situations.

Notice, too, that the Power Thank You doesn't just make the other person look good. It also makes *you* look good to everyone involved by showing that you have empathy and humility and that you care. It also shows that you can be trusted to give credit where it's due—something that can win you important allies in a corporate world where people too often get burned by disloyalty.

To make this an even more effective approach, offer your Power Thank You in a group setting if you can. The larger the audience for your words, the more striking their effect will be.

■ THE POWER APOLOGY

While my daughter Lauren taught me the importance of a powerful thank you, my daughter Emily helped reinforce the lesson that you can't buy people off cheap when you've hurt them.

It started with a phone call from my wife, who said, "You're in big trouble!" The reason: I'd failed to show up for seven-year-old Emily's dance class. "She kept looking for you, and you weren't there," my wife said. "I think you need to talk to her. I wouldn't want to be in your shoes."

I immediately thought "bribe/distraction" and went to the store and bought Emily a cute doll with arms and legs that twisted like pipe cleaners. When I arrived home, my wife pointed me in the direction of my daughter's room. I sat down on Emily's bed and said, "I promised you that I would come to your dance practice and didn't come, isn't that so?"

Emily fought a losing battle to hold back the tears, straining her mouth open and trying to look up at the ceiling. I continued, "I made a mistake and I'm sorry and I will tell you this. I will never make a promise to you again that I don't keep. I want you to believe that a promise from your dad is something you can always count on. As a result I will not make you many promises. Instead I'll say, 'I'll try,' and then hope I surprise you more often than not."

I hugged her and then gave her the doll, and she gave me a hug in return. But the day after our talk, I found the doll in the garbage can in her room. Hurt? I was, a little. But I also had to grin. My little girl, in her own way, was telling me: "I'm important, buddy, and you'd better know it. You can't buy me off easy—and you'd better keep your promise."

I did keep that promise faithfully, and in turn Emily forgave me completely—in time. But it didn't happen overnight, and it took lots of effort on my part to win back her trust.

My guess is that somewhere along the line, you'll screw up too—and it might be over something bigger than a recital. Maybe you'll betray the trust of a colleague, or fail to come through on a big project, or hurt a partner or child by saying terrible words you can't take back.

If so, understand this: Merely saying "sorry" will patch over the wound, but it won't heal it. That's because your screw-up wasn't just a blunder. It was also a suggestion that the other person doesn't matter (creating a huge mirror neuron gap), and you're responsible for proving otherwise. So don't just say you're sorry; if the situation warrants it, offer a Power Apology.

A Power Apology consists of what I call the "4 Rs." They are:

Remorse: Demonstrate to the other person that you know you caused harm and you are truly sorry. For example: "I know I made you look bad in front of the boss by failing to bring the documentation you needed to make your case for the new computers. It was my fault he turned down your request and everyone has to use the old computers for another year."

When you're doing this, allow the other person to vent and don't become defensive even if the person is over the top. When you encourage people who are furious to get their anger off their chests, it speeds the healing process.

Restitution: Find some way to make amends, at least partially. For example: "I know the whole team is pissed off about not getting the computers, and they blame you. I'm going to go to each team member and explain that it's my fault. I can't undo the damage, but at least I can take the blame off your shoulders."

Rehabilitation: Demonstrate through your actions that you've learned your lesson. If a mistake occurred because you didn't do your job right or you shot off your mouth without thinking, do whatever it takes to avoid making the same mistake in the future.

Requesting forgiveness: Don't do this immediately, because actions speak louder than words. To truly earn forgiveness, you need to sustain your corrective actions until they become part of who you are. At this point—and not before—go back to the person you've hurt and say, "Are you able to forgive me for hurting you?"

Most people will accept a Power Apology graciously because they'll respect your humility and your efforts to prove yourself worthy of their trust. Even people who initially wrote you off—"I don't want anything to do with you ever again!"—will usually be willing to forgive (even if they don't totally forget). This is a particularly good way to heal the wounds that often result from a bitter divorce.

If someone doesn't forgive you even after you've done all you can to make amends, don't assume that you're unforgiveable; instead, realize that you may be dealing with someone who's unforgiving. If that's the case, don't drive yourself nuts over it. Just let it go, and don't work up a grudge that'll add to your emotional baggage.

If your Power Apology works, on the other hand, make good use of your second chance—and recognize that this approach works only once. Betray a person's trust a second or third time, and you're beyond redemption. Stick to your promises, however, and eventually you'll fully restore the trust the person once placed in you—and possibly even make it stronger.

➡ *Usable Insight*

The more often you say *and* sincerely mean "thank you," the less you need to pay your people. The more often you say *and* sincerely mean "I'm sorry," the quicker your people will get back to work.

➡ *Action Step*

Think of (a) the person who's helped you the most over the last month, (b) the person who's helped you the most over the past year, and (c) the person who's helped you most over your lifetime. Offer each one a Power Thank You, either in person or by mail or e-mail.

Now, think of a person you've hurt, let down, and never made amends to—and give that person a Power Apology.

It's never too late to give a Power Thank You or Power Apology, if you really mean it.

FAST FIXES FOR 7 CHALLENGING SITUATIONS

The techniques you now know are like martial arts moves: potent on their own, but even more powerful when you combine them. In the following chapters, I'll show you examples of ways to tackle some common but hard-to-handle situations (and one scary one) using a mix of the skills you've learned—plus a few bonus tricks.

24

THE TEAM FROM HELL

Good management consists of showing average
people how to do the work of superior people.
—JOHN D. ROCKEFELLER,
INDUSTRIALIST AND PHILANTHROPIST

*SCENARIO: The good news is that my boss just put me in charge of
my first major project. The bad news is that the team I'm managing
is mostly—how do I put this politely?—a bunch of losers. One guy,
Jonas, is really smart, and I think I can count on him to come through.
But I'm also stuck with Dirk, who's two years from retirement and
wants to do the least amount of work possible. My lead analyst is
Linda, who'll spend half her time at the water cooler complaining
about everyone. And Sherry, the fourth member of the team, is senior
to me and probably wanted my assignment, so I'm expecting some
hard feelings. As a new and inexperienced manager, I don't have a
clue where to start. Help!*

F irst, realize that you—and many other managers these
days—are dealing with "silos": people who are self-
involved, thinking only of themselves, and working
less and less cooperatively. That's especially true if you're in a field
where rampant mergers and layoffs have shredded any sense of corporate or interpersonal loyalty.

As long as your team members stay in their silos, your job will be next to impossible. That's because these people will fail to share information, resulting in major mistakes and wasted effort. They'll refuse to share their expertise, making everyone's job harder. And when things get tough, they may even fall into a pattern of sniping or outright sabotage.

So the first thing you need to do is to break down the thick walls between these silos. To do that, build on the things all silos have in common: the sky above (a shared vision) and the ground below (shared values).

Step 1 in this process is to hold a meeting with your team. Your goal at this meeting is to increase your team members' sense of passion, enthusiasm, and pride in your project, so use a variant of the PEP Challenge I outlined in Chapter 9. Start out like this:

> *You are all outstanding professionals and highly skilled at what you do, and I'm lucky to have you on our team.*
>
> *Unfortunately, like nearly all professionals these days, we've all turned into silos to focus on what we need to do. The good news is that this allows us to function well in our own areas; the bad news is that it makes it more difficult for us to work synergistically and cooperatively.*
>
> *To beat the competition, we need to work seamlessly together like an NBA Championship team, World Series winner, Super Bowl winner, or gold medal–winning Olympic team.*
>
> *What gets superstars on those teams to work together and beat other teams is that they lower the competitiveness among the individuals on their own teams.*
>
> *Right now, our company and I need you to work together like one of those winning teams. So we're going to build on what silos have in common, besides big walls between each other.*
>
> *The two things silos have in common are the sky above—which is a shared vision we all believe and enthusiastically buy into—and the ground below —which is the shared values we all want to honor and live by. Every winning team has the shared vision of winning a championship and the shared value of flawless execution.*
>
> *So let's take the time to clarify what those are for all of us. . . .*

In the discussion that follows, zero in on the key elements of the PEP Challenge. Let people talk about what vision they're passionate about and how this project is part of achieving it. Let them talk about what they're enthusiastic about when their team is buzzing and productive, and what they're proud of (or not proud of) about the company. Draw out comments about the changes they want to see to feel more passionate, enthusiastic, and proud about what they're doing. As you do this, you'll feel your team's initial apathy or hostility gradually morph into excitement and energy.

Of course, that's just Step 1—because once this excited and revved-up team leaves the room, they'll still be Jonas, Dirk, Linda, and Sherry, and they'll still have issues with you and each other. Ignore these issues, and soon your inspiring words will fade away and everyone will hunker down in their silos again.

To prevent that, figure out what you need to do to reach each team member and make that person think, "I care about this project and I want to do my best." Some suggestions:

1. **Keep Jonas happy.**

Jonas is self-motivated, so don't ride herd on him. Instead, stay out of his way—and acknowledge his value by employing the Power Thank You at strategic times. For instance, in a status meeting where the bigwigs are in attendance, say, "Great news—we're actually ahead of target. Last month things looked pretty rocky, but Jonas worked overtime and pulled off a couple of major miracles to solve the supply problem. Thanks to him, we're exceeding our goals."

Also, remember that the best thing you can do for talented and motivated workers like Jonas is to remove obstacles, which includes toxic people. So for God's sake, don't pair him up with Linda.

2. **Make Dirk feel needed.**

If Dirk's like most workers edging toward retirement, he can still get plenty fired up. You just need to supply the spark.

To do that, let him know he's valuable—because lots of older employees feel underappreciated or shoved aside, especially if they're working under a young manager. So say things like, "You have the most experience with this software—is it okay if the younger team members rely on you as a mentor?"

Also, let Dirk know you find him interesting and intelligent by asking transformational questions like: "With your experience, what do you see as the most important thing our division could do in the future to add value to the company?"

If Dirk continues to be a low achiever, take him out to lunch and use the Fill-in-the-Blanks approach ("I'm guessing that you sometimes find your work frustrating because _____"). Odds are you'll uncover a problem you can solve together.

3. **Make Linda feel important.** Remember what I said earlier about making annoying people feel valuable? That's your ticket with Linda. In addition to Linda's regular duties, assign her a task that you specify is *very* important. Make sure, however, that this task doesn't interfere with the rest of the team. In fact, if you can, give Linda a task that *benefits* the whole team so she'll invest more heavily in its success.

For example, say, "Linda, with our tight schedule I need to be sure that we all have exactly what we need to work fast. You're so organized that I'd like to make that your responsibility. So every Friday, I'd like you to check very quickly by e-mail with each team member and then meet with me for 10 minutes at 3:00 and tell me if anyone needs equipment or support. This is really important, so everyone make sure you e-mail Linda with your list of needs on Friday."

When Linda comes to you with her info (for instance, "Jonas says he needs somebody to test circuit boards"), say something like, "Okay, I'll handle that right away—and thank you. I know you need to take time away from your own work to check with everybody each week—so if you like, I'll ask the people who are allocating responsibilities for you to free up some of your time. We really need you to keep us all on track." Again, this encourages her to buy into the success of the whole team.

If Linda doesn't reform and continues to carp and complain, consider using the "Do you really believe that?" question to stop her complaints. ("I overheard you saying that your team members are idiots and we'll never meet our goals. Do you really believe that?") Or try the Empathy Jolt—for instance, by asking her, "How do you think Dirk feels when you criticize him for being slow?"

4. **Get Sherry's secret out in the open.** Your boss probably had a very good reason for giving this project to you and not Sherry,

so don't feel insecure about it. However, since you both know that she's senior to you and she probably expected this assignment, a little stipulation can help clear the air.

For instance, say, "Sherry, I'm especially grateful to you for the hard work you're putting in on this project. I know I'm newer and less experienced than you, and some people in that position would resent having me as their manager, but you've been really supportive. I've learned a lot from watching you, and I think it'll make me a better manager." (That's a stipulation and a Power Thank You all rolled into one—extra points!)

When you acknowledge Sherry's secret thought—*"Why is this upstart getting my job?"*—and defuse it with your graciousness and humility, Sherry will be far more willing to leave her silo and join your team.

Oh, and one last word of advice: Stop fretting over being new and inexperienced and recognize that you got this job because you're good. Project confidence, and you'll inspire confidence. Project insecurity, and everyone will sense it. (Or, as the diplomat and presidential candidate Adlai Stevenson once put it: "It's hard to lead a cavalry charge if you think you look funny on a horse.") So assume that you're the best manager your company has ever had—and then go out and prove it.

➡ **Usable Insight**
Assemble the best team you can, and then become the person they—and you—would want to lead them.

➡ **Action Step**
If you currently manage a business team, list your team members' names on a piece of paper. Go down the list and identify two kinds of "silos": The "grain silos," who quietly put in their eight-hour days aloof and alone, and the "missile silos," who sit hunkered behind their walls ready to shoot down any perceived offender. Approach these individuals one by one, and see how many are willing to lower their walls when you address them with empathy, humility, and a sincere willingness to understand them.

25

CLIMBING THE LADDER

The secret of getting ahead is getting started.
—AGATHA CHRISTIE, MYSTERY AUTHOR

SCENARIO: I work as a mid-level manager in a multinational corporation. I think I can go places in this company, but I'm not sure how to make people notice me. I'm about to be transferred to a different department—is there a way to impress my new boss?

S tart on Day 1 by using the question I mention in Chapter 19: "What are the three things I should *always* do and the three things I should *never* do to do well in this job?" Immediately, you'll stand out from the crowd.

Next, realize that your success depends on getting the people under you to perform—and that's going to happen only if you communicate successfully with them. Since these people are strangers to you, use the Side-to-Side technique (see Chapter 20) liberally in your first few months. This is the fastest way to figure out what your subordinates are doing, how well they're doing it, and where potential problems lie. When you detect problems, defuse them rapidly using the appropriate tools from Section III.

One thing your boss will want to know is: "Can this person handle the pressure of a management position?" You'll look like a leader if you deal with crises without falling apart, so practice the "Oh F#@& to OK" drill in Chapter 3 religiously. If you're the one who stays in control when everyone else is falling apart, you'll earn the respect and confidence of the people above you.

At annual reviews, make it clear that you're invested not just in your own success but also in the success of your company and your boss. For instance, if your boss asks if you have questions, say something like this: "I want you to imagine we are meeting for my next review and you tell me, 'You exceeded our expectations with regard to your results, your attitude, and even with some innovative solutions that really helped our company and me.' What can I do to make that scenario occur?"

When opportunities arise, ask transformational questions that will deepen your relationship with your boss. For instance, ask, "How do you see the company changing as a result of technological advances?" or "What do you see as our most important goals and obstacles?" Questions like these tell your boss that you see him or her as more than just a person with a bigger paycheck than you.

Also, look for occasions to make your boss "feel felt." The higher up managers are, the more stressed and less "felt" they feel. That's because unlike coworkers at the same level (who don't hesitate to say to each other, "You look tired" or "Are you okay?"), managers and subordinates tend to stick to professional talk (and it can be lonely at the top of the organizational pyramid). Don't be overly familiar, but also don't hesitate to occasionally say things like "Six meetings in two days—how do you stand it?" or even, if the person looks weary or sad, "Are you feeling okay today?" That little bit of empathy can create a powerful stir of gratitude.

If you're really serious about getting ahead, here's another tip: Look beyond your immediate boss. Are there other people, either inside or outside the company, who could help you climb the corporate ladder? If so, take my advice: Kiss up to them. I don't mean that in a bad way, but in a good way. These people are intelligent and can offer guidance and open doors for you, and many of them enjoy serving as mentors.

Early in your career, find out who are the most powerful, respected, successful, *and* emotionally guarded people in the industry or field you are most passionate about. (You'll find some good ideas for meeting these movers and shakers in Chapter 30.) Find a way to develop a relationship by saying to them, "I want to learn everything you know. What's the best way to do that?" Then do whatever they ask or tell you, learn everything they know, and learn how to be trusted and indispensable to them. Because the old saying is true: It's good to have friends in high places.

➡ *Usable Insight*
Visualize yourself in the job that you want; then actively plan to get there.

➡ *Action Step*
Make a list of the 10 people you most admire in your company. Using the techniques you've learned (and the information in Chapter 30), see if you can think of ways to become closer to one of these people and position him or her as a mentor.

26

THE NARCISSIST AT THE TABLE

The customer is sometimes wrong.
—HERB KELLEHER, FORMER CHAIRMAN AND CEO,
SOUTHWEST AIRLINES

SCENARIO: I work for a product design and development company. One of our clients asked us to develop packaging for a line of personal care products, but the project is turning into a nightmare. One week, the client needs the shampoo bottles designed first. The next week he says, "I need the bath oil bottle designs immediately," so we drop the shampoo bottles (not literally!) and start on the bath oil bottles—only to hear the next week, "It's urgent that we get the soap bottles going." But he still wants the shampoo and bath oil bottles done instantly as well! We can't finish a single element of the project because every week the client changes his demands. And our boss is no help because she just repeats that old line, "The customer is always right." My take: The customer is wrong, and we're eating up all our profits because we're working less efficiently and it's taking too much time. Is there a way to handle this?

our client is that common animal, the Classic Narcissist. He doesn't care if he's making your life miserable, cutting into your profit margin, or getting you in trouble with the boss. He wants what he wants—and he wants it now, now, now.

Narcissists are pretty common in the business world (many visionary leaders and CEOs of start-ups fall into this category) and you'll also run into average people who exhibit narcissistic behavior because they think it's a good way to get ahead in the corporate world. So be prepared to meet your share of both true narcissists and pseudonarcissists, and be ready to handle them. (Not sure if you're dealing with a narcissist? See the quick test in Chapter 11.)

In your current situation, you obviously can't expect a solution to come from your boss. In fact, judging by her lack of concern for your needs, she's probably a bit of a narcissist herself (or too weak to stand up to a client). So it's up to you. As I explained in Chapter 11, you can't change a narcissist—but sometimes you can tame one. If you're handling the communications with your client, here's what you do.

The next time you meet with your client, wait for him to make another demand with his, "Now, everyone stop what you're doing and listen to me!" style of interruption. Quietly allow him to lay his new demand on the table. At that point, say very calmly and in a positive way, "Excuse me, but before we continue, you do know that if we listen to you and drop whatever we're doing now, we won't be able to finish that task—which was critically important to you last week. So I need to clarify which task you'd like us to do now: the task you thought was top priority last week, or the task you think is top priority this week."

This approach will bring your narcissist to a halt, because it's no longer you versus him. Instead, it's his former self versus his current self. When he can't create a win-lose situation in which you lose and he wins, he'll need to come up with a workable demand instead.

Be careful, however, to use this approach only with difficult, demanding, narcissistic clients. In most cases when problems arise, they occur not because anyone's being unreasonable or narcissistic but because there's a misunderstanding between you and the client. When that happens, the best approach is to go deep using the "Hmmm" technique I laid out in Chapter 17. For example, if a client looks at your brilliant design and says, "We hate it—it's terrible!" don't overreact. Instead, say "Hmmm . . ." or "Tell me more." This will quickly calm your client, allowing you to get past "It's terrible!" and identify the specific problems that usually are far short of catastrophic. You can also use the Fill-in-the-Blanks technique by saying, "You're unhappy with this design because you imagined it being more _____." By making your client feel felt and understood, these approaches can lead to a quick resolution.

In your case, however, your boss's failings make it likely that you'll be dealing with more than your share of difficult clients. One way to lessen problems with these clients is to use the Stipulation Gambit to let them know up-front that there are realistic limits to what you can do. For instance, start a relationship with a demanding client like Mr. Shampoo Bottle by saying something like, "I do want you to realize that we work best if you give us specific ideas and allow us time to develop them fully. We're flexible but we are a very small firm, and we can only do our best if we have a clear idea of what you need." Then get the client's ideas and priorities in writing, so you'll have a paper trail to back you up.

More important, see if you can get your boss to comprehend this simple fact: The more irrational demands you try to satisfy for a narcissistic client, the less time you'll have to take care of good clients who treat you fairly. Keep the narcissists under control, and you'll make the good clients happier. And that makes sense—because the nice guys are the clients you really *want* to keep.

➡ *Usable Insight*
Good clients and customers raise the bar. Bad ones just keep hitting you over the head with it.

➡ *Action Step*
Analyze your work schedule to determine how many extra hours per month you spend catering to difficult clients. Now, determine how much extra service you could provide to good clients if you rein in the troublesome ones. This will give you the courage you need to face the narcissistic clients down.

The best approach is to try to surround yourself with as many decent, appreciative, low-maintenance clients as you can. Doing so will cause you to become increasingly disgusted with the narcissists In your life—and that will give you the courage to cut your losses with them.

27

STRANGER IN TOWN

The successful networkers I know, the ones
receiving tons of referrals and feeling truly
happy about themselves, continually put the
other person's needs ahead of their own.
—BOB BURG, AUTHOR, *THE SUCCESS FORMULA*

SCENARIO: I run a printing firm, and we're new in town, so I need to drum up business. I've joined the Chamber of Commerce and even serve on some of its committees, but it's not bringing in very many new clients. Is there a better way to network?

I'm guessing that you started a printing business because you're good at printing—not at passing out business cards or making "cold calls." In fact, your efforts at marketing yourself probably seem pretty hit-or-miss right now, with a lot more misses than hits.

Surprisingly, however, it isn't that complicated. Dr. Ivan Misner is the founder of BNI, the most successful referral organization in the world. Misner, who's studied networking for more than 20 years, says that effective networkers either consciously or intuitively apply what he calls the VCP Process®. Here's how it works.

Visibility, Misner says, is the first phase of growing a relationship. Visibility is where you and another individual become aware of each other, perhaps because of your PR and advertising efforts or perhaps through someone you both know. You may become personally acquainted and work on a first-name basis, but you know little about each other.

Credibility is the quality of being reliable and worthy of confidence. Once you and your new acquaintance begin to form expectations of each other, and the expectations are fulfilled, your relationship can enter the credibility stage. If each person is confident of gaining satisfaction from the relationship, then it will continue to strengthen. Credibility grows when appointments are kept, promises are acted upon, facts are verified, and services are rendered.

Profitability is the phase of the relationship when it becomes mutually rewarding. Do both partners gain satisfaction from it? Does it maintain itself by providing benefits to both? If it doesn't profit both partners, it probably won't endure.

Now, here's how to use your new skills to succeed in all three stages of Misner's VCP Process.

■ THE VISIBILITY STAGE

At this point, don't simply tell people who you are—tell them why they'll like you and why they'll want to be your friends or clients.

At those Chamber of Commerce meetings, for instance, remember the most important rule of all: Be interested rather than interesting. Talk about other people's businesses more than yours. Ask smart questions about what people do, how they do it, and what marketing strategies work for them. Never, ever cut them short when they're talking; instead, ask questions that will motivate them to say more.

Next, make other people feel felt. If they bring up problems ("the city is killing our business with that street repair project"), show that you care—even if the problems don't affect you at all. Go out of your way to understand other people's issues and help solve them, and you'll impress them with your generosity.

You can also jump-start new relationships by asking transformational questions that show others that you value their intelligence. For instance, ask another business owner, "What effect do you think the redevelopment project will have on our businesses five years from now?" or "Where do you see this city's economy going over the next decade?"

Last but not least, use the Power Thank You to create good will. If another business owner has a great idea that contributes to the success of your business or your networking organization, point it out publicly in a meeting ("Chaz saved us $500 by loaning us the tables for the art festival—an extremely generous act that helped bring the event in under budget—and he spent hours with his staff setting the tables up at 5 A.M."). Your gratitude will create mirror neuron empathy with the other person, making that person want to reciprocate—possibly by using your firm or referring other people to you.

■ THE CREDIBILITY STAGE

At this stage, it's absolutely crucial to avoid creating dissonance in your new relationship. You're still getting to know each other, and each fact the other person learns about you assumes great importance. So present yourself honestly and accurately, don't make false assumptions about what the other person wants or needs, and don't make any promises you can't keep.

Also, make the other person feel valued. Go out of your way to perform acts that aid the other person, and to acknowledge any help you receive (using a Power Thank You when it's appropriate). If you can, be the first person in the relationship to offer a referral . . . and if the person refers someone to *you,* go to extra lengths to satisfy that client.

In short, don't focus on what's in it for you. Instead, focus on what's in it for your new friend. And work very hard not to screw things up—but if you do, use the Power Apology to make amends for your mistake.

■ THE PROFITABILITY STAGE

When you reach this point, keep focusing on making your new contact feel interesting, valuable, and understood. However, also consider the advice I offered in Chapter 11 about ridding your life of toxic people. Typically, your new contacts will fall into three categories —givers, takers, and reciprocators—and you want to weed out the takers early on. So review your list of new contacts and focus your efforts on the givers or reciprocators while easing the takers out of the picture. Be generous with your new contacts and don't keep score, but give priority to relationships with people who are willing to give back.

Above all, relax and let your network grow over months or years. Relationships, especially ones that lead to mutual profitability, take time, so try not to be impatient. (In fact, the more you try to speed up the process, the more you'll turn people off.) Know, too, that it's okay if not every relationship pans out. Sometimes you have to kiss a lot of toads before you find a prince—or a whole network of them.

➡ *Usable Insight*
  Focus on "What's in it for them?" and reciprocators will sooner or later ask, "What can I do for you?" Focus on "What's in it for me?" and they'll ask themselves, "How do I make this person go away?"

➡ *Action Step*
  If you dread networking, ask yourself what you'll gain from it. What's the compelling vision that makes it worthwhile to go outside your comfort zone? Maybe it's your goal of owning a successful business, or your plan to win a promotion. Or maybe it's your desire to feel proud of yourself for overcoming your fears and putting yourself out there. Keep that vision firmly in front of you, and it'll translate into commitment and action.

28

THE HUMAN EXPLOSION

Every little thing counts in a crisis.
—JAWAHARLAL NEHRU, FIRST PRIME MINISTER
OF INDIA AFTER ITS INDEPENDENCE

SCENARIO: I work in a high-pressure financial business where millions of dollars are on the line every day. To add to the pressure-cooker atmosphere at our office, management is sending many of our jobs offshore. People are really stressed out and scared about losing their jobs and lots of them seem to be on a hair trigger. Frankly, I think there's the potential for one of those "disgruntled employee goes berserk" scenarios, and I'm not sure how I'd handle it.

Y ou're not alone. These days any one of us—manager, CEO, doctor, teacher, attorney—can be a target for a person who reaches the breaking point and totally loses control.

Scary? You bet. (Just ask any psychiatrist, because we all deal with such short fuses.) And I won't lie to you: You can't always handle an extremely upset or violent person. Often, the only option you have is to run or hide. But if the person isn't an immediate threat, or if there's no way to escape, the right words can give you the power to bring a situation under control—or possibly even save a life.

The key fact to know when somebody goes nuclear is that the person is stuck in attack mode, so *rational, reasonable, intelligent conversation won't work.* A guy who's throwing a computer at the boss or waving a gun around can't listen to reason, because he can't access the higher thought processes that say "Hey, calm down—this is crazy."

In case you skipped Chapter 2, here's why: In a time of crisis, a person's brain decides whether to put the logical upper brain or the primitive lower brain in charge. If it chooses the primitive brain, it locks out the smart brain.

Your task, if you're facing a person who's running amok, is to break that lock. How? By talking the person up gradually from "I want to hurt someone" to "I'm terribly upset" to "I need to find a smart way to handle this." These stages correlate with the three levels of the brain: the primitive reptile brain, the emotional mammal brain, and the logical human brain.

To get an out-of-control person to act sanely, you need to move the person up gradually through all three levels *in order.* (Think of it as "rapid evolution.") Here's how to do it.

Stage 1

At this point, your goal is to move the person up from the primitive reptile brain to the emotional mammal brain. To do that, follow these steps:

1. Say, "Tell me what happened."
Venting allows the person to begin moving from blindly striking out (the most primitive response) to feeling emotional (a higher response). The person's screaming or yelling will upset you, but it's far less dangerous than the threat of physical violence—so let it happen.

2. Say, "I need to make sure that I heard exactly what you said, so I don't go off in some wrong direction. If I heard you right, what you said is. . . ."
Then repeat exactly what the person said, calmly and with no angry or sarcastic inflection in your voice, and say, "Is that correct?" When you do this, you mirror the person—that power-

ful connecting technique I talk about in Chapter 2. You also cause the person to move from venting to listening, which slows the brain down so the person can think more intelligently.

3. Wait until the person says *"Yes."*
The simple act of saying "Yes" causes the person to move in the direction of agreement rather than hostility. "Yes" also indicates a willingness to pull away from acting out. If the person corrects what you've said in any way, repeat the information you're given.

4. Now say, "And that makes you feel angry/frustrated/ disappointed/upset or what exactly. . . ."
Pick the word you think best describes what the person feels. If the person corrects you, ask the person to say what the actual feeling is and repeat it back and get another "Yes." Remember that *when someone attaches a word to a feeling, it lowers agitation.* That's critical.

Stage 2

At this point, you're dealing with someone who's no longer striking out wildly but is still venting—better, but still a problem. So your next goal is to move the person from the emotional middle (mammal) brain up into the rational upper (human) brain. Here's how you do it.

1. Say to the person, "And the reason it's so important to fix this or make this better *now* is _____ ."
This fill-in-the-blanks technique requires the person to think of an answer, which opens the door to the reasoning (human) parts of the brain. One important tip: When you make this statement, emphasize the word *now* to show that you understand the urgency of the person's need.

2. Illuminate the path out.
If the person fills in the blank by saying, "Because if things don't change, I'm going to explode, hurt myself, punch someone," etc., follow with, "Really. . . . Please keep talking so I make certain I really understand this" (said without question or sarcasm, but in a way to emphasize that you are really listening).

Then say, "If that's the case, let's figure out how to get through this so you don't do something that will make a really bad situation worse. I know we can, because you've been here before and you got through it. In fact, while we're at it, let's figure out a solution so you never have to get to this place again."

This shows that you've heard the person, you take the problem seriously, you recognize how bad the person feels, and you're committing to help solve the current crisis and prevent similar problems in the future. All of this makes the person feel less alone—what I call a "The Lord is my shepherd" experience.

At this point the person will look to you as a guide to salvation, and the crisis can move toward resolution—preferably with the help of professionals trained to deal with crisis situations. The problem is far from solved, but everyone can *start* to solve it now that the worst is over.

■ WHY DO PEOPLE SNAP? ■

Nearly all the violence that we hear about in the media is triggered by rage, and more specifically, by impotent rage. Impotent rage results when a person feels rejected and humiliated by people and feels powerless to do anything about it. Having few effective internal coping skills, the person explodes and lashes out at the world.

You and I feel enraged and impotent at times, too. Unlike us, however, violent people can't handle these emotions. Scientists report that chemically and structurally, many violent people are "wired" for impulsive anger and poor self control. Sociologists note that many of them suffered abuse as children. And psychologists and psychiatrists cite violent people's lack of *object constancy*.

Object constancy is the ability to retain a positive attachment to another person even if you're disappointed, hurt, or angry with the person. Violent people have an extremely low tolerance for frustration and lose all emotional and psychological connection with anyone who upsets them. When that connective link breaks, people become objects to be destroyed in the same way as one might smash a tennis racket on the ground following a lousy shot.

Remember this if you're ever dealing with a violent person, because it'll help you avoid the potentially deadly mistake of appealing to the person's compassion ("I know you don't want to hurt me"). Instead, focus all of your efforts on appealing to the person's self-interest.

➡ *Usable Insight*
If someone can't or won't listen to you, get him to listen to himself.

➡ *Action Step*
If you know that someone in your life is on a hair trigger and might go off at any minute, prepare for a possible crisis by practicing the steps I've outlined in this chapter until they become second nature. If possible, practice them with another person who can play the out-of-control person's role. This will help you prepare mentally for having an angry or emotional person in your face, which can be highly alarming and trigger your own primitive instincts if you're not prepared. Also, practice the "Oh F#@& to OK" drill I outline in Chapter 3.

29

GETTING THROUGH TO YOURSELF

Don't find fault. Find a remedy.
—HENRY FORD, INVENTOR

SCENARIO: Every New Year's Day I make a list of resolutions I know I'll fail to keep. I promise myself I'll exercise every day. I promise myself I'll stop acting like a shrew when my kids act up. And then there's that resolution about going back to school to get my MBA. I feel disgusted when I look at my out-of-shape body in the mirror, guilty when I think about how I'm not living up to my career goals or my expectations as a parent, and frustrated by my mounting pile of broken promises to myself—but work and life keep getting in the way, and it's so hard to follow through on my plans and goals. Do you have any suggestions?

S ure. To begin with, use the Empathy Jolt—on yourself. To understand why, picture yourself saying something like this to your very best friend: "You know, I really love you . . . but your body sure isn't perfect. Look at your disgusting, flabby upper arms! When's the last time you worked out? And frankly, the way you scolded your son about forgetting to mow the lawn the other day—jeez, you're a nasty shrew. And while we're at it, what's with that bare spot on the wall where your MBA degree should be? What a complete failure you are at everything."

Would you say any of these things to someone you love? Of course not. When it comes to talking to yourself, however, there's no limit to how brutal you can be. Just look at the self-criticism contained in your comments: You've told me you're disgusted with yourself, you're a shrew, and you're sure you'll fail. Keep talking to yourself that way, and guess what? You probably *will* fail.

Want to succeed instead? Then try something different. Next time you have a quiet moment, ask yourself this question: "What's holding you back from accomplishing your goals, and how frustrating is that for you?" (If talking to yourself in this way is too difficult, imagine a person who cares about you asking this question.)

Then listen to your own answer. It probably goes something like this.

- "I want to go back to school but it means taking time away from the kids—so I do what seems right for my family, but sometimes I feel like I'm cheating myself."
- "I try to handle my kids' problems maturely, but sometimes I lose my temper because after a stressful day I desperately need some comforting and all I get is selfish attitude. And it hurts when I work so hard to take care of them and all I hear is complaints."
- "It's really hard to motivate myself to exercise when it's 8 P.M., the dishes aren't done, and my daughter needs help with her math homework."
- "All of this frustrates me because no matter what I accomplish, I feel guilty about what I *don't* accomplish."

When you do this mental exercise, it'll open your eyes to the fact that you're not a failure. Instead, you're human. You're juggling dozens of responsibilities, you're suffering from a serious mirror neuron gap thanks to your kids (especially if they're teens!), and you're making compromises because you're a caring and giving person. So give yourself a break. In fact, give yourself credit for the 3,000 things you're doing *right*.

Your quick but powerful Empathy Jolt will clear away the guilt that's keeping you from taking a clear look at your goals. Remember how I talked in Chapter 4 about rewiring your brain to see people in a new way? The same is true of goals: Sometimes we pick them for the wrong reasons (for instance, "My father will be disappointed if I don't become a doctor," or "Everyone in my family has a PhD") and then never reexamine them. Other times our lives evolve while our goals stay stuck, and we need to get the two in sync.

As you analyze your goals, avoid falling into the expectation trap—that is, the idea that "This has to happen (or not happen) for me to be happy or successful." For example, you're kicking yourself for not getting your MBA yet—but do you *need* to get your degree right now in order to be successful or happy? Or could you take a different path—for instance, getting your degree online over the next few years—and be just as fulfilled?

And don't confuse "reasonable" with "realistic." Reasonable means "makes sense." Realistic, on the other hand, means "likely to happen." For instance, it may be reasonable to decide on January 1 that you're going to sign up for your MBA classes, never yell at your kids again, and start running marathons—but it's probably not realistic. It typically makes more sense to pick one goal that's likely to be attainable and focus on it.

When you have that goal in mind, use this approach to achieving it:

- **Set specific targets.** I tell clients to write a step-by-step plan. Like plotting waypoints on a GPS before a trip, this helps you visualize the road you need to follow.
- **Put your goal in writing.** Describe exactly what you need to *start* doing and what you need to *stop* doing in order to succeed. Putting your words on paper strengthens your commitment to achieve your goal.
- **Tell someone about your goal.** Call a person you respect, explain the change you want to make in your life, and ask the person to either call or e-mail you every two weeks to see how you're doing. Your desire to keep this person's respect will be a powerful motivator to keep your commitments. If you do this, remember to give your helper a Power Thank You for assisting you, and also find a way to return the favor.

- **Keep toxic people from stopping your progress.** Review Chapter 11 and identify any problem people who lower your resolve or weaken your confidence. If possible, avoid them as you work toward your goal.
- **Give it time.** If you're breaking unproductive habits or creating good ones, keep this rule in mind: It takes between three and four weeks for a new behavior to become a habit, and it takes about six months for that habit to become second nature. Be patient with yourself.

If you want to break bad habits, you can also use the Never Again Tool I outlined in Chapter 21. For instance, if you've just had another blow-up with your daughter about unfinished chores, here's what your Never Again Tool might say:

1. If I had *that* to do over again, what I would do differently is:

Instead of yelling at Jamie for not doing her chores, I would try the Empathy Jolt by asking her, "If Spot could talk, what do you think he'd say when he's really hungry and he's really hoping for dinner and you walk right out the door without feeding him?" or "What do you think your dad would say if I asked him what it's like for him when he comes home from work really exhausted and he can't rest because you forgot to do the dishes and he has to do that chore for you when he really needs to relax for a few minutes?" (It's not guilt tripping; it's empathy training.)

If that doesn't work, I could try the Reverse Play. For instance, I could say to Jamie, "I know I'm always complaining about your chores or your homework or your clothes, but I know I don't always do a perfect job as a mom—so instead of going through a list of my complaints, I want to apologize for the times when I screw up. Here are the things that I think bother you about me. . . ." If I use this approach, I may create enough empathy to make Jamie want to do more for me in return.

2. I would do things differently because:

Yelling at Jamie doesn't work. It just makes her start yelling back, and instead of solving the problem I make everyone in the house unhappy.

3. On a scale of 1 to 10, my commitment to do this the next time is: 10.

4. A good person to hold me accountable for doing this would be:

Doug, because he gets just as frustrated as I do when Jamie doesn't do her chores but he also hates coming home after work to a house where everyone is mad and stressed out—so handling this problem is very important for him too.

As I mentioned in Chapter 1, we're all unique, so experiment with different approaches for getting through to yourself. For instance, give the Impossibility Question a try. Say to yourself, "I agree that this is impossible. Now, what would make it possible?" When you come up with an answer, run with it.

Above all, as you tackle your goals and work on building more effective habits, avoid a second type of expectation trap. If you *count on* something and it doesn't happen, you'll be devastated. If you *expect* it and it doesn't happen, you feel a sense of failure or loss. But if you *hope* for it and work toward it while realizing that it might not occur (or might take a little longer than you thought) you'll enjoy your victories and view setbacks with a sense of perspective that will keep you on track to your goals.

■ THE SIX-STEP PAUSE ■

Often we're derailed on our way to our goals by our own impulsive behavior. Here's a little trick—a close relative of the "Oh F#@& to OK" drill in Chapter 3—that can help you avoid making a misstep that could keep you from reaching your personal or career goals. I call it the Six-Step Pause, and it walks you up from your snake and rat brain to your human brain. Here's how it works.

When you feel yourself starting to go astray—for instance, if you're ready to explode at a colleague whose support you're trying to win, or you're on the sixth day of quitting smoking and you're thinking of running to the store for cigarettes—follow these six steps:

1. **Practice physical awareness.** Identify sensations like tension, a pounding heart, a craving, or lightheadedness. Pinpoint them and give them a name. This will help you control them.

2. **Practice emotional awareness.** Attach an emotion to the sensations you're feeling. For instance, say to yourself, "I'm very angry" or "I'm desperate." Naming your feeling will help prevent the amygdala hijack I talk about in Chapter 2.

3. **Practice impulse awareness.** Say to yourself, "This feeling makes me want to _____." Being aware of your impulse will help you resist it.

4. **Practice consequence awareness.** Answer this question: "If I follow through with this urge, what is likely to happen?"

5. **Practice solution awareness.** Complete this sentence: "A better thing to do would be. . . ."

6. **Practice benefit awareness.** Say to yourself, "If I do that better thing the benefits will be. . . ."

By the time you get through these six steps, you'll know what you need to do to stay on course and avoid a potentially disastrous meltdown—and you'll be calm enough to listen to your own advice.

This is also a terrific tool to use to talk your children through their upsets. Get in the habit of doing this when they're young, and they'll internalize it into their personality. This will help them stay cool, calm, and collected under pressure when they're older.

➡ *Usable Insight*
During tough times, say unto yourself what those who care about you would say unto you . . . and then believe it. Otherwise, you are dishonoring the love they feel for you.

➡ *Action Step*
Here's a fun thing to try if you're the kind of person who has trouble acknowledging your strong points: Let someone else do it for you. When you're talking with someone who admires you, ask the person this question: "So, what exactly do you admire about me?" When the person replies, reflect on his or her words and savor them. Then, after a moment, respond, "Wow! Thank you (pause)— anything else you admire about me?" The deeper you go, the more vitality (and gratitude) you'll feel, and the more energized you'll be when you get back to tackling your goals.

30

Six Degrees of Separation

To succeed in your career, it's less important
what you know or even who you know than
who truly *knows* you and *how* they know you.
—IVAN MISNER, FOUNDER, BNI

SCENARIO: I work in marketing, and I'd love to lure some big clients to our firm because I think that's the fastest road to promotion. However, I have no idea how to make contact with the rich and famous. Is it even possible for a "nobody" like me to get past the layers of staffers who surround powerful people these days?

If you're in client development, sales, or marketing, you have a tough job: getting total strangers to listen to you. That job is even tougher if you need to reach powerful people who are fiercely guarded by dozens of gatekeepers.

Cold calling and other techniques for reaching strangers are worthy of an entire book—and yes, I'm working on it right now! But in the meantime, here are a few quick tricks that can move you rapidly from six degrees of separation to zero.

■ CREATE ONE-ON-ONE SITUATIONS

First, use the approach I employed to introduce myself to Tom Stemberg of Staples (see Chapter 6). Powerful people frequently participate in seminars and panel discussions, and they usually call for questions at the end of their talks—so go to these meetings and ask the right questions. When you get your shot, remember that your job is to make your targets sound interesting and to ask questions they want to answer. Your goal is to make these people look good—thus creating mirror neuron empathy and encouraging them to reciprocate—so don't blow it by trying to show off.

To increase your odds of success, attend charity benefits, book signings, or other functions where you have a chance to come face to face with a VIP. If you're creative, you can always find a way to make this person "feel felt"—even at a very public event—and if you accomplish this, you'll create an instant bond.

On one occasion, for instance, I was a keynote speaker at the Association of Corporate Growth's annual conference in Beverly Hills, California. The night before the conference, speakers had a chance to meet each other at a cocktail party held at the hotel. The most successful of the speakers was Mike Heisley, the Chicago-based billionaire and owner of the NBA's Memphis Grizzlies and a man who's responsible for turning around many companies. Everyone clearly wanted his attention, and they formed a long line to greet him. When I met him I asked him: "What did you learn about success from your dad?"

Mike paused, proceeded to stop speaking with other people (much to their dismay), and spontaneously pulled out two chairs and invited me to sit down with him. He then started talking about how his dad taught him to make deals based on the best interest of everybody, not just his own interest. He told me, "My dad had so much faith in me to succeed without taking advantage of anyone that I wanted to honor his belief in me. My dad made me want to be a better man, and I like to think I have."

By realizing that leaders often learn valuable lessons about how to behave (or not behave) from their parents, I'd granted Mike the opportunity to reexperience the gratitude he felt toward his dad. That warm feeling made him open to hearing from me after the conference.

■ MAKE VIRTUAL ALLIES

Meetings, however, aren't the only forum in which you're zero degrees of separation from your quarry. Thanks to the Internet, you can touch a powerful or famous person online—especially if you remember the core rule that people want to feel felt.

One way to do this occurred to me after my first book, *Get Out of Your Own Way,* was published. At that time, I discovered that writing a book is like having a baby: You hope it's intelligent, attractive, and well received, but you never know. You also tend to check the reviews of your book—probably too often—to see what the world is actually saying about you. In addition, you click on blog posts and discussion groups that talk about your brainchild. I discovered first-hand the hurt feelings that an occasional negative or even mean-spirited review can create. On the other hand, when someone really understood where I was coming from, it was very uplifting.

Not long after I became aware of these narcissistic but very natural feelings, a friend sent me a copy of *The Confidence Course* by *Parade* magazine CEO Walter Anderson. My friend told me that I'd like it, and that I'd also like Walter Anderson. My friend was right. What's more, I went to Amazon.com and noticed that no one had written a review of this wonderful book.

So I wrote the first one—not just a quick "loved it, recommend it" note, but one in which I invested time and thought. I'd learned from Walter's book that he hadn't enjoyed as close a relationship with his father as he would have liked. That resonated with my experience with my own dad, and I told Walter I admired how he'd demonstrated a fatherly caring for his readers when he'd never received that caring himself. My words came straight from my heart, but actually touched him deep in his. As a result, Walter and I now have a relationship.

Virtually all people—no matter how powerful—"ego surf" the Net, and there's no gatekeeper standing between you and them online. I know it's hard to imagine glamorous celebs or incredibly powerful business leaders sitting around in their pajamas typing their names into Google, but believe me: They do.

■ REACH THE GATEKEEPERS

If you're cold calling, of course, you won't reach a VIP easily because you'll run into the gatekeeper blockade. That's why it's crucial to establish a relationship with the person whose job it is to block your path. Make that person your ally rather than your enemy, and you can reach the VIP just about any time you want.

To do that, recognize that:

■ The gatekeeper is crucially important to the VIP's success and deserves recognition.
■ The gatekeeper is probably just as interesting as the VIP, and will appreciate you recognizing that.
■ The gatekeeper is probably suffering from severe mirror neuron gap, because all day long he or she gets flak from disgruntled people simply for correctly doing the job of protecting the boss (who probably isn't very grateful).

Armed with these facts, you're ready to gain entry into many a VIP's fortress. Take, for example, this two-minute ice-cold call I made to the assistant of one of the most powerful CEOs in America. (For obvious reasons, I've changed names and other identifying information.)

"Hello, is this Joanne?" I asked on the telephone.

"What?" she replied.

"Is this Joanne Nelson?" I continued.

"Who is this?" she responded.

"Is this the *famous* Joanne Nelson that Ted Burke wrote about and thanked in his bestseller, *Leader of the Pack?*" I persisted.

"Yes, WHO is this?" Joanne replied, half annoyed and half amused.

"This is Dr. Mark Goulston, I'm a psychiatrist, author, and writer and . . ." I started, whereupon Joanne jumped in.

"Boy! Could we use someone like you around here!" she vented.

"Relax, Joanne. It'll be okay. Take a deep breath," I replied in my clinical voice.

"YOU relax! YOU try dealing with a crazy person all week long," she continued, now on a roll.

"Joanne, it'll be okay. You have to deal with only one. I deal with a different one every hour. I hope you still have a personal life?" (I asked this question because I know that most personal assistants to powerful CEOs have little or no time for a life of their own.)

"What personal life? I don't even have time for a real dog. I have a ceramic cocker spaniel that's by my door," she continued.

"Well, I understand they're very good with children," I continued the banter.

"Want to know his name?" she replied, not missing a beat.

"Sure," I said.

"His name is Sit," she answered, whereupon we both laughed.

I continued the conversation by explaining that I'd written an article I thought her boss would like and that his editor had given me this number. After our call, I wrote Ted the following letter, which I enclosed along with my article, knowing full well that Joanne would read my missive.

> *Dear Mr. Burke,*
>
> *One of the first things I am going to do when I become rich is to hire someone like your assistant, Joanne, to protect me from people like me. She was helpful, fun, and yet guards access to you like a pit bull.*
>
> *I hope she knows how valuable she is to you and that you don't make the same mistake that I sometimes do of failing to appreciate those people who make my life possible, because I'm having to deal with those who make it impossible. If so, you of all people should know better.*
>
> *Etc.*

I called four days later to follow up to see if my letter had arrived, and said, "Hello, Joanne, this is Dr. Goulston again. I don't know if you remember me; we spoke a few days ago."

"I remember *you*," Joanne replied warmly and playfully.

"I wondered if Ted had received my package," I continued.

"Yes, Dr. Mark, we received it and I sent it on to where he is on vacation—that is, except for the letter," she answered.

Feeling a little nervous, I interjected, "Oh?"

"Yes—I took that letter out and READ IT TO HIM over the phone!" she said triumphantly.

As a result of my call and my letter, Joanne and I have become good friends and if I want access to Ted, she's happy to put me through.

So there you have it: several great techniques for reaching the people you thought were unreachable. All of these methods are simple (if you have enough courage). And all rely on three basic rules: Make people feel interesting, make them feel important, and above all, make them "feel felt."

Why do they work? Because underneath the glamour and the money and the power, VIPs and their staffs—just like everyone else—are just people. And you can reach just about *any* person, as long as you're willing to try.

➥ *Usable Insight*
Inside the most untouchable VIP who's wary of being "hit on" is a person who's aching to be touched in just the right way.

➥ *Action Step*
What person do you most admire and most want to meet? Search the Internet for locations where the person is speaking, and see if you can get an invitation. Or, if the person has a book out, use Amazon or other review sites to post a "power review" of the book. If you have a blog, use it to post your thoughts about how the person has changed your philosophy or your life. Also use social and business networking sites such as Facebook, Plaxo, LinkedIn, and Twitter to make positive comments.

AFTERWORD

One key to reaching people is to be reachable yourself, and I'm always delighted when my readers reach out to me. If you implement the techniques in this book, I'd love to hear how they work for you. You'll also find more communication tools and ideas at www.markgoulston.com.

And one more thing before I go: Thank You! As you know by now, I'm big on giving a Power Thank You to anyone who makes my life better. By taking a chance on reading this book and having the courage to change your life by using the information you've learned, you've given me the biggest reward a psychiatrist can achieve: the feeling that I've made a positive difference in your life. I hope you'll find your new knowledge as powerful and beneficial as it's been for me, and I wish you great success at work, at home, . . . and everywhere.

INDEX

Abuse, 207
Acknowledgment, 167
    in Power Thank You, 181
    transactions instead of, 157
Action step
    with crisis, 208
    with dissonance, 86
    with "Do you really believe that?,"
        141
    with Empathy Jolt, 131
    with exhaling, 76
    with feeling felt, 53–54
    with fill-in-the-blanks, 175
    with goals, 214
    with "hmmm . . .," 148–149
    with Impossibility Question, 115
    with interest, 63
    with listening, 43–44
    with Magic Paradox, 121–122
    with narcissism, 199
    with networking, 203
    with "Oh F#@&" to "OK," 35
    with Power Thank You, 185
    with promotion, 196
    with Reverse Play, 137
    with Side-by-Side, 169
    with stipulation, 154
    with taking it to no, 179
    with team-building, 193
    with toxic people, 108
    with transformational questions,
        162
    with value feeling, 68
    with VIPs, 220
    with vulnerability, 93

Advanced Medical Optics, 27–28
Affinity, 165
Alzheimer's, 18
Amazon, 217, 220
Americans with Disabilities Act, 151
Amygdala, 16–17
Amygdala hijack, 17, 18, 70, 73
Analogy, 129–130
Anderson, Walter, 217
Anger, 126, 145
Annual reviews, 195
Apology, 184
Appreciation, 181–183
Argument, 86
    questions instead of, 166–167
Association of Corporate Growth, 216
Attack, 145
Awareness, 213–214

Bailey, T. Lee, 99–100
Bennis, Warren, 55–56, 86
Benson, Herbert, 74
Blaming, 122–124, 127
Borderline personality disorder, 98
Breathing, 32
Bullying, 99–102
Burke, James, 27
Business 2.0, 56–57
Buy-in, 7, 8–9
    from Impossibility Question, 113

Coca-Cola, 176
Cold calls, 200
Cold War, 48
Collins, Jim, 56–57

Compassion, 208
Competitiveness, 190
Confidence, 193
The Confidence Course (Anderson), 217
Control, 179
Conversation deepeners, 165
Conversation-stopper, 167
Credibility, 201, 202–203
Crisis
    action step in, 208
    fill-in-the-blanks in, 206–207
    frustration in, 207
    "Oh F#@&" to "OK" for, 208
    scenario, 204
    usable insight with, 208
    venting with, 205–206
    yes in, 206
Criticism, 79–80
    as conversation-stopper, 167
Cultural differences, 85–86
Customer service, 145–146

Debate, 73, 74
Deep listening, 55–56
Defensiveness, 50, 74–75, 127, 145
    "hmmm . . ." instead of, 148
    from lecturing, 164
    in Power Apology, 184
    from questions, 171
Defusing, 147–148
Dialogue, 144, 158
DiClemente, Carlo, 8
Disappointment, 137
Discomfort, 150–151, 154
Dissonance
    action step with, 86
    corporate, 83–84
    examples of, 77–78, 79, 83–85
    fill-in-the-blanks instead of, 171–172
    identification of, 80–81
    in marriage, 79
    in networking, 202

perceptions causing, 80
    unavoidable, 85–86
    usable insight with, 86
Distress, 70–71
"Do you really believe that?," 138, 192
    action step with, 141
    examples of, 139–141
    usable insight with, 141
Dunn, Walter, 176

Edge, 19
Education, 39–40
Emotions, 39–40
    exhaling through, 73
    preparation for, 208
    self-control with, 28–29
    violence and, 207–208
    words with, 31–32, 206
Empathogenic communication, 126
Empathy, 19, 117
Empathy Jolt
    action step with, 131
    examples of, 124–126, 127–129
    for goals, 209–211
    with habits, 212
    usable insight with, 131
    use of, 127–129, 192
    on yourself, 130–131, 209–211
Encouragement, 142–144
Enthusiasm, 83–84, 85
Escalation, 144, 147–148
Evans, Lieutenant, 5, 6–7
Examples
    of amygdala hijack, 18
    of dissonance, 77–78, 79, 83–85
    of "Do you really believe that?," 139–141
    of Empathy Jolt, 124–126, 127–129
    of exhaling, 69–70, 71–74
    of feeling felt, 45–47, 48, 49–50, 51–53

of Fill-in-the-Blanks, 170–171, 172–174

of "hmmm. . . . ," 142–144, 145–146, 147, 148–149

of hostage negotiators, 4–7

of Impossibility Question, 112, 113, 114

of interest, 55–58, 59, 60–63

of listening, 36–38, 41–43

of Magic Paradox, 116–117, 118–119, 120–121

of mirror neuron gaps, 20–21

of "Oh F#@&" to "OK," 30–31, 34–35

of parenting, 10–12

of Power Apology, 183

of Power Thank You, 180, 181–182

of public speaking, 21–23

of Reverse Play, 132–133, 134–136

of self-control, 27–28

of Side-by-Side, 163–164, 166–167, 168

of stipulation, 151–154

of taking it to no, 176, 177–179

of toxic people, 97–98, 99–100, 101–102, 107–108

of transformational questions, 155, 157–161

of value feeling, 66–67

of vulnerability, 87–89, 91–93

Exhaling

action step with, 76

through emotions, 73

examples of, 69–70, 71–74

in parenting, 75–76

usable insight with, 76

venting and, 73–74

Exhaustion, 73–74

Expectations, 201, 211

Eyes-to-the-sky, 161

Fear, 16–17, 203

Fearful aggression, 33

Feedback, 20–21, 65

Feedforward, 82

Feeling felt

action step with, 53–54

examples of, 45–47, 48, 49–50, 51–53

in networking, 201

for promotion, 195

usable insight with, 53

Ferrazi, Keith, 91–92, 95

Fight-or-flight response, 15, 74

Fill-in-the-blanks, 177

action step with, 175

in crisis, 206–207

examples of, 170–171, 172–174

instead of dissonance, 171–172

for problem-solving, 199

in team-building, 191–192

usable insight with, 175

for yourself, 173–174

Filters, 37–41, 43

First impressions, 37–41

Forgiveness, 91, 184–185

Friendships, 134–136

Frontal cortex, 16–17

Frustration, 156–157

in crisis, 207

Fuhrman, Mark, 99

Gardner, John, 57

Gatekeepers, 218–220

Gender, 39–40

Generation, 39–40

Gestures, 172

GGNEE model, 39–40

Goals

action step with, 214

Empathy Jolt for, 209–211

expectations with, 211

Impossibility Question with, 213

scenario, 209

steps for, 211–212

toxic people and, 212

Goals (*continued*)
  usable insight with, 214
Goldsmith, Marshall, 82
Goleman, Daniel, 17
Good to Great (Collins), 57
Gorbachev, Mikhail, 48
Goulston, Emily, 183
Goulston, Lauren, 180–181
Grain silos, 193
Grudges, 135–136
  after Power Apology, 185
Guests, 66–67

Habits, 212
Hard sell, 177
Hare, Robert, 104–105
Heisley, Mike, 216–217
Henry, Patrick, 62
Hibbard, Dave, 111
"Hmmm . . ."
  action step with, 148–149
  examples of, 142–144, 145–146,
    147, 148–149
  instead of defensiveness, 148
  for problem-solving, 198–199
  usable insight with, 148
Hollander, Edward, 103
Hostage negotiators
  emotions and, 28
  example of, 4–7
  shared activities for, 164
Hostility, 148
Humility, 86
  in Power Apology, 185
Hyperbole, 139, 141

Ignorant blamers, 123–124, 130–131
Impossibility Question
  action step with, 115
  buy-in from, 113
  examples of, 112, 113, 114
  with goals, 213
  in personal life, 115

usable insight with, 115
Interest
  action step with, 63
  examples of, 55–58, 59, 60–63
  questions showing, 60–63
  usable insight with, 63
Internet, 217–218
Interview
  questions in, 155–156
  stipulation in, 151–152

Kicking but, 111
Kissing up, 195
Kramer, Detective, 5–6, 12

Lawyers, 150
The Leadership Institute, 55–56
Lecturing, 164
Lieberman, Matthew, 31
Listening, 39
  action step with, 43–44
  deep, 55–56
  examples of, 36–38, 41–43
  in public speaking, 21–23
  usable insight with, 43
The Lord is my shepherd experience,
    207
Loyalty, 182, 189

Macaque monkeys, 1–19
Magic Paradox
  action step with, 121–122
  examples of, 116–117, 118–119,
    120–121
  trust from, 119–121
  usable insight with, 121
Mammal brain, 15–16, 205–207
Managing by walking around
    (MBWA), 165
Marriage, 79
Mazzo, Jim, 27–28
MBWA. *See* Managing by walking
    around

Mentor, 174, 195–196
Middleton, Rick, 38–39
Miller, William R., 8
Mirroring, 19–23
    with gratitude, 202
    of vulnerability, 90–91
mirror neuron gaps, 57, 65, 90
    with appreciation, 182
    example of, 20–21
    of gatekeepers, 218
    satisfaction of, 157
Mirror neurons, 19, 150–151
Misner, Ivan, 200–201
Missile silos, 193
Mistakes, 50, 174, 177
Monolog, inner, 161
Motivation, 191–192
Motivational Interviewing (Miller and
    Rollnick), 8
Muskie, Edward, 34
"My Golden Rule" (Collins), 56–57

Narcissism
    action step with, 199
    prioritization with, 198, 199
    scenario, 197
    stipulation with, 199
    in toxic people, 103–104, 137
    usable insight with, 199
Nationality, 39–40
Neediness, 95–98
Networking
    action step with, 203
    dissonance in, 202
    fear of, 203
    feeling felt in, 201
    Power Apology in, 202
    Power Thank You in, 202
    prioritization in, 203
    scenario, 200
    toxic people in, 203
    transformational questions in, 201–
        202

usable insight with, 203
value feeling in, 202
VCP Process® for, 200–202
"The Neurology of Self-Awareness"
    (Ramachandran), 19
Never Again Tool, 173–174
    with habits, 212–213
No, taking it to
    action step with, 179
    examples of, 176, 177–179
    usable insight with, 179

Object constancy, 207
"Oh F#@&" to "OK"
    action step with, 35
    for crisis, 208
    examples of, 30–31, 34–35
    for promotion, 195
    speed drill, 32
    usable insight with, 35

Paranoid delusions, 20–21
Parenting, 10–12, 75–76
Passion, 83–84, 85
Patience, 203, 212
PEP CEO Challenge, 83–85
    for teams, 190–191
Pepsi, 176
Perception, 40–41
    as dissonance cause, 80
Persuasion Cycle, 7–9
Pharmaceutical representative, 159–
    161
Physicians, 159–161
Positive phrasing, 173
Powell, Colin, 34–35
Power Apology
    defensiveness in, 184
    example of, 183
    grudges after, 185
    humility in, 185
    in networking, 202
    trust and, 183–184, 185

Powerlessness, 79–80
Power Thank You, 183
  acknowledgment in, 181
  action step with, 185
  examples of, 180, 181–182
  in networking, 202
  in team-building, 191
  transacting instead of, 181
  usable insight with, 185
Prefrontal cortex, 32
Pride, 83–84, 85
Primate brain, 15–16
Prioritization
  with narcissism, 198, 199
  in networking, 203
Privacy, 48–49
Problem person, 43–44
Problem-solving, 147
  fill-in-the-blanks for, 199
  "hmmm . . ." for, 198–199
Productivity, 169
Profitability, 201, 203
Promotion
  action step with, 196
  feeling felt for, 195
  "Oh F#@&" to "OK" for, 195
  scenario, 194
  Side-by-Side for, 194
  transformational questions for,
    195
  usable insight with, 196
Proschaska, James, 8
Psychopaths, 104–106
Public speaking
  example of, 21–23
  listening in, 21–23
  transitioning in, 153–154

Questions, 165. See also Impossibility
  Question; Transformational
  questions
  defensiveness from, 171
  direct, 171
  instead of argument, 166–167
  in interview, 155–156
  to show interest, 60–63
  for VIPs, 216

Ramachandran, V. S., 19
Reaction phase, 30, 32
Reagan, Ronald, 48
Realism, 211
Reasonableness, 211
Recenter phase, 30, 32
Reengage phase, 31, 33
Referrals, 202
Reflection, 161–162
Refocus phase, 31, 33
Reframing, 174
Regberg, Scott, 138–139
Regberg & Associates, 138
Rehabilitation, 184
Reinforcement, 173
Relationship deepener, 145
Relaxation, 73–74
  during stipulation, 153
Relaxation response, 74
Release phase, 30, 32
Remorse, 184
Repetition, 205–206
Reptile brain, 15–16, 205–206
Resistance, 4, 144
Respect, 167
Restitution, 184
Reverse Play
  action step with, 137
  as diagnostic test, 136–137
  examples of, 132–133, 134–136
  with habits, 212
  usable insight with, 137
Rollnick, Stephen, 8

Sabotage, 190
Scenario
  crisis, 204
  goals, 209

narcissism, 197
networking, 200
promotion, 194
separation, 215
team-building, 189, 191–193
Self-assurance, 63
Self-control, 30
with emotions, 28–29
example of, 27–28
Self-defeating behavior, 173
Self-motivation, 191
Separation, 215
Shared activities, 164
Shared values, 190
Shared vision, 190
Side-by-Side, 165
action step with, 169
examples of, 163–164, 166–167, 168
for promotion, 194
usable insight with, 169
Silos, 189–190, 194
Six-Step Pause, 213–214
Skepticism, 152
Slackers, 132–134
Socrates, 165
Socratic Method, 165
Speed, 29–31
Stemberg, Tom, 62–63
Stevenson, Adlai, 193
Stipulation, 192–193
action step with, 154
to avoid discomfort, 150–151
examples of, 151–154
with narcissism, 199
relaxation during, 153
usable insight with, 154
Stress, 29–31. *See also* Distress
Stress hormones, 75
Stuttering, 151
Subordinates, 194
Supportiveness, 108
Suppressing, 70, 76
Syncing, 25

Takers, 102–103
Team-building, 190
action step with, 193
fill-in-the-blanks in, 191–192
Power Thank You in, 191
scenario, 189, 191–193
transformational questions in, 191–192
usable insight with, 193
Teenagers, 75–76
Telling, 165
Threats, 16–17
Three-part brain, 15–16, 205–207
Toxic people, 94
action step with, 108
bullies, 99–102
examples of, 97–98, 99–100, 101–102, 107–108
goals and, 212
narcissism in, 103–104, 137
needy, 95–98
in networking, 203
psychopaths, 104–106
self-diagnosis, 106–108
takers, 102–103
usable insight with, 108
Transactions, 155–156, 158–161
acknowledgment instead of, 157
Power Thank You instead of, 181
Transformational questions, 156
action step with, 162
examples of, 155, 157–161
in networking, 201–202
for promotion, 195
in team-building, 191–192
usable insight with, 161–162
Transitioning, 153–154
Transtheoretical Model of Change (Prochaska and DiClemente), 8
Trust
with expectations, 201
with giving credit, 182

Trust (*continued*)
  from Magic Paradox, 119–121
  Power Apology and, 183–184,
    185
  violation of, 166
Tylenol, 27

Urgency, 206
Usable insight
  with crisis, 208
  with dissonance, 86
  with "Do you really believe that?,"
    141
  with Empathy Jolt, 131
  with exhaling, 76
  with feeling felt, 53
  with fill-in-the-blanks, 175
  with goals, 214
  with "hmmm . . .," 148
  with Impossibility Question,
    115
  with interest, 63
  with listening, 43
  with Magic Paradox, 121
  with narcissism, 199
  with networking, 203
  with "Oh F#@&" to "OK," 35
  with Power Thank You, 185
  with promotion, 196
  with Reverse Play, 137
  with Side-by-Side, 169
  with stipulation, 154
  with taking it to no, 179
  with team-building, 193
  with toxic people, 108
  with transformational questions,
    161–162
  with value feeling, 68
  with VIPs, 220

  with vulnerability, 93

Value, feeling of, 64–65, 191, 192
  action step with, 68
  examples of, 66–67
  in networking, 202
  usable insight with, 68
  venting with, 65–66
VCP Process®, 200–201
Venting
  in crisis, 205–206
  exhaling after, 73–74
  value feeling with, 65–66
Very Important People. *See* VIPs
    (Very Important People)
The View, 113
Violence, 204–205
  emotions and, 207–208
VIPs (Very Important People)
  action step with, 220
  gatekeepers to, 218–220
  Internet and, 217–218
  questions for, 216
  usable insight with, 220
Visibility, 200–202
Vulnerability
  action step with, 93
  assertive, 90, 93
  examples of, 87–89, 91–93
  mirroring of, 90–91
  usable insight with, 93

Weaknesses, 150–151
What Got You Here Won't Get You There
    (Goldsmith), 82–83
Williams, Mr., 71–72

Yes
  cascade of, 117–119
  in crisis, 206

ABOUT THE AUTHOR

Mark Goulston, M.D., is a business psychiatrist who through his early career intervened with suicidal and violent individuals. This eventually led to his training of hostage negotiators for the police and the FBI. From this experience he developed an uncanny ability to get through to virtually anyone, and the methods he used form the basis of *Just Listen.* Along with that, he made house calls to dying senior executive patients and their families, during which he helped people resolve disputes at the eleventh hour. Family members then brought him in to work with their family companies, which is when Dr. Goulston's work crossed over into the business world.

Over the last 25 years, Dr. Goulston has worked with middle-market to Fortune 1000 companies and with boutique to national law and CPA firms, teaching them the listening skills to get through and break down silos both internally and externally. Internally, this resulted in more transparency, a freer flow of information, and more nimble and resilient organizations. Externally, when facing clients, boards of directors, and shareholders of companies, this enabled the organizations to shorten their sales cycles, effectively and consistently communicate their values and value propositions, and ultimately succeed in the marketplace.

Dr. Goulston's unique insight on interpersonal and communication challenges coupled with his 30-plus years as a clinical psychiatrist have enabled individuals, teams, and organizations to achieve their full potential.

His list of past and present clients includes Goldman Sachs, IBM, Federal Express, Xerox, Accenture, Deutsche Bank, Bloomberg, Kodak, Merrill Lynch, Wells Fargo, Bank of America, the Office of the Los Angeles District Attorney, the Los Angeles Police Department, and the FBI.

Dr. Goulston has been a professor at UCLA's famed Neuropsychiatric Institute for more than 25 years and was selected as one of America's Top Psychiatrists in 2009, 2005, and 2004 by the Washington, D.C.–based Consumers' Research Council of America.

He is a bestselling author whose books include *Get Out of Your Own Way* with coauthor Philip Goldberg, and *Get Out of Your Own Way at Work*. He writes the Tribune syndicated column "Solve Anything with Dr. Mark" and writes and contributes content to the *Harvard Business Review, The Huffington Post,* and *Fast Company.* He is frequently asked to share his expertise with national print and broadcast media, including *The Wall Street Journal, Fortune, Newsweek, Time,* Reuters, NPR, CNN, Fox News, and the *Oprah* and *Today* shows..

KEYNOTES/WORKSHOPS

Dr. Goulston presents keynote speeches and workshops on each of the following topics.

* **"Just Listen": The New Secret Weapon for Getting Through to Absolutely Anyone**
  If you really want to get through to people, what you tell them is less important than what you enable them to tell *you*. Discover the simple tools to do this and get through to anyone.

* **Avoiding Something or Someone? How to Confront Anyone About Anything, Anywhere, Anytime**
  It's not that people don't *want* to confront people, it's that they don't know how to do it in a way that won't be painful. Dr. Goulston will show you how to confront anyone in any situation in a way that will *never* make the situation worse, and in most cases will make things considerably better. Once you learn these secrets to pain-free confrontation, you will be able to spontaneously deal with anyone about any troubling situation —whether the problem is current, or whether the situation is with someone with whom a confrontation is long overdue— freeing you up to move successfully into the future.

* **Be Courageous**
  Stay too long in your comfort zone and you'll end up safe . . . *and sorry*. Why? Because you will be one of the countless people who regret much more what they *didn't* do than what they did. Discover how to change that now and grab life by the horns!

* **Potential IS a Terrible Thing to Waste—How to Get Out of Your Own Way (and Help Others Do the Same)**
Calamity is unavoidable, but tragedy is not. One of the greatest tragedies in life is to reach the end only to discover that life was less—or *much* less—than it could have been, that what you could have avoided you failed to prevent, and what you could have achieved you didn't, only because you weren't able to get out of your own way. Dr. Goulston shows you how to do just that: overcome the self-defeating behaviors that are holding you back—and help others do the same.

* **The Best Life Possible—How to Make It Happen**
What are the chances that you will get to the end of your life with no regrets? If you want to increase the odds of that happening, you'll want Dr. Goulston to show you how to live your life without regrets.

* **Breaking Down Silos**
Whoever said "The World Is a Ghetto" was wrong. The world is a *silo*. And unless you find a way to break down the walls that separate the people within your company, and that separate you from your clients, customers, and investors, your company will never be able to innovate, cooperate, collaborate or perform at its peak. In this highly interactive/experiential presentation, Dr. Goulston will help you break down silos, and you will then be able to connect, collaborate, and interact with people more effectively than you could ever have imagined.

Contact Mark Goulston for more information.

Websites: http://markgoulston.com
          http://justlistenthebook.com

email: info@markgoulston.com

Free Resources: http://markgoulston.com/resources